THE "M" WORD

A Collection of Stories about
Miscarriage *and* Hope

EDITED BY
PAMELA DJIMA

ISBN: 978-1-4834-8661-1 (sc)
ISBN: 978-1-4834-8660-4 (e)

Rev. date: 10/12/2018

Contents

Acknowledgements

To my big sister—Thanks for encouraging me as a writer. I appreciate the fact that you have always been willing to proofread my work and provide me with meaningful feedback. One day, I will repay you by taking you along to my Barnes and Noble book signing in New York. Afterwards, we shall toast each other from crystal glasses as we dine in a Michelin-starred restaurant and reminisce about back in the day when we were young girls with big dreams. Truth be told, you have been a constant source of encouragement since the 80s. Thanks for everything.

To my Pops—I think you genuinely believe that I can do anything. The words that you have spoken so often still ring in my ears: "It's not beyond you." Thank you for helping to build a sense of audacity in me. The fearlessness you worked to establish has served me well.

To my husband—Thank you for encouraging me to persevere with this project. Your ideas and suggestions have been invaluable.

To all the brave women who have shared their story in this book—Thank you so much for your openness and honesty. Without you, this book would be significantly shorter. It would probably be more of a pamphlet than a book. Thank you for your willingness to be so candid about such a sensitive subject matter.

To all the friends who helped find people willing to share their stories for this book—Thank you. Your contribution was priceless.

To Bethany Eden—Thank you for producing such brilliant artwork for the front cover of this book. I appreciate your flexibility and the gracious way in which you accommodated the evolving vision.

Thank you to everyone who said that this project was a good idea.

Your words of encouragement were like the gentle tapping on a bird's cage that emboldens it to leave the comfort of its former home and take flight into the unknown.

To my Heavenly Father—Thank you for the hope that I have in Christ and for the assurance that in the midst of every storm, I always have a very present help in time of need.

Introduction

This book is not intended to be a dossier outlining ten things that you absolutely must do in order to adequately heal from a miscarriage. In this text, you will find no detailed prescriptions regarding how to "bounce back" after your loss. On the contrary, this book is born from a firm belief that it is important for every one of us to document our stories even if these stories are painful or uncomfortable.

Some of our stories are beautifully wrapped up and adorned with an elaborate bow. In such instances, the account may read, "I had one miscarriage and then I had six healthy children and now life is great." I like these stories and they are significant because they remind us that every cloud has a silver lining and that greatness really can come after devastation. However, these are not the only important narratives. There are some tales that are still in the process of unfolding, and thus, they remain a work in progress. Scores of people are still on the journey of believing and trusting God for a child after many years of disappointment. Their stories may not yet possess a neat conclusion; nevertheless, these narratives are dynamic and worthy of being told.

I am a strong believer in the candid documentation of our stories for two main reasons. First, it helps to expose the lie. In a world where communicating via social media is the norm, it is commonplace to believe the fallacy that everyone else has it all together. It is easy to focus on the highlights that are presented—the weddings, the births, the new jobs, the stylish outfits, and the lavish holidays—and conclude that everybody else's life is perfect. The reality is this: everybody experiences difficulties. These hardships are not the same for us all but they are challenges nonetheless. Honest sharing is the enemy of isolation and engenders a sense of solidarity that is a foundation of true healing.

That's not all though. Candid sharing does more than expose the lie—it also serves to encourage hope. Hope can be defined as the belief that regardless of how dire the current circumstances are things will get better. The power of hope is not to be underestimated. I know, from both personal experience and the tales of the survivors who have walked before me, that an individual can conquer pretty much any adversity life throws at her so long as she possesses hope. When we are willing to openly share our stories despite our discomfort, a beautiful thing happens. It creates the possibility for hope to be inspired. If I know that once upon a time, you walked through tragic circumstances and yet somehow you are still here today, it gives me hope that although I may currently be in the midst of a living nightmare, life can be better.

So in this book you will find a group of Christian women who have poured out their hearts. The result is a collection of stories that are open and candid. Each of these women is at a different stage on the journey of Faith. Yet, we are united by a common Hope in Jesus Christ and by the fact that we have all chosen to document truth.

My Journey with My Jesus and Pregnancy

Annabelle

"God don't like ugly," they say, but He loved mine.

I suppose my journey started with pregnancy and is still surrounding pregnancy. I became a born-again Christian in 2001. I had been involved with the Catholic Church but felt that Christianity would rule my life and thus was not for me. I considered myself a good person whose sole aim in life was not to intentionally hurt anyone. However, the older I got, the more I began to feel the sting of human relationships. I eventually found myself pregnant at the age of 20. I was in my first year at university and in a relationship with someone who loved me and had given me his heart. However, my heart was wrapped up with someone else. The solution to this problem was to remove the factor that would change my life forever—the baby. I understood that this was my right and that the baby was not even real and did not have a voice. So off I went and terminated the pregnancy. This led to many years of depression, insomnia, and emptiness.

You may be wondering, *What's the connection between me, this loss, and the Lord?* Well, when I felt that I was no longer able to manage my very destructed life, the Lord came in and poured out His restoration, removed shame, and led me to the life that I have as a born-again Christian, nearly fifteen years later. Since then, I have married a godly

1

Christian man, who has also been subject to the suffering that relates to pregnancy loss.

I have been fortunate enough to have been pregnant seven times. A brief summary of my history is as follows: I have experienced one ectopic pregnancy, one stillbirth at 25 weeks, one full-term pregnancy, and one pre-term pregnancy that resulted in giving birth at 26 weeks. This premature birth was followed by the baby enduring a three-month hospital stay before she could finally be brought home. After all this, I did not conceive for four years. Then, within twelve months, I had two miscarriages. One was an "unidentified pregnancy of unknown location." The other was a late miscarriage at 20 weeks.

I have always wondered about my future concerning family, mainly because when I was saved, all I wanted to do was live for the Lord. I had grand plans of flying off to China to become an English teacher. So when I eventually met my husband, having a family was an afterthought, a consequence of being in love and wanting to expand our family. However, I did not know that I would experience such a turbulent journey. I feel that in order to be able to share God's grace about everything that has happened, it is important to speak briefly about God with regard to each loss.

Prior to getting married, my husband and I did not keep our relationship away from promiscuity and I found out that I was pregnant in 2009. My periods had been very irregular. When I noticed that I had missed a period, I did a home pregnancy test. The test was positive. This pregnancy was not planned and happened at the wrong time once again. I was still living at home and we had only just completed our civil marriage ceremony. I began to bleed and when I had a scan, the sonographer was unable to detect the yolk sac. The pregnancy was identified as a suspected ectopic pregnancy. I had to have numerous blood tests before the doctors decided to give me a chemical drug to remove any pregnancy developing outside of the womb. Although I didn't expect to be pregnant, I was now a Christian striving to live right before God. My husband and I had been recently married and were trying to maintain our integrity. However, I was convinced that this result was a judgement for us not living holy whilst dating. I felt grieved about having to have this medical intervention and knowing that the pregnancy would end and there would be no baby. I remember the night that the hospital called and said that I would have to come into the hospital as my HCG levels were not doubling as they should. I had to tell my family and my husband's family. My mother was furious. Nevertheless, I checked into hospital, was given a drug, and was home by the following Monday. However, I had a really bad reaction and had to be readmitted to hospital because I passed out. I received this loss as judgement. Looking back, I did not grieve but instead accepted the situation as exposing my hidden life and actions, and viewed the loss as the consequence of this.

After this, we recognized that we were both disappointed that we were not able to have this baby, and I was able to recognize my husband's longing for a child. We didn't plan to conceive straightaway but we didn't try to stop it from happening either. Then in May 2010, I found out that I was pregnant again. I was overwhelmed, overjoyed, ecstatic, and any other word that you can use. I would wear clothes to show off a two-month (non-existent) bump. I felt confident in this pregnancy as we were married, living together, working, and hopefully pleasing before God.

One evening in my sixth month of pregnancy, my work colleagues were having a team dinner and they asked if I would come. I felt that the Holy Spirit was telling me not to go, but I went anyway. *It's just a harmless meal*, I thought and so I went. That weekend I had food poisoning. My water broke and I delivered my Joshua Michael at exactly 25 weeks. He was stillborn. My heart was broken. I went into hospital thinking that if he comes early, it is OK because they can look after him as a premature baby. I was reassured by the hospital staff that they had found his heartbeat. However, when the scan was performed, I was told that there was in fact no heartbeat. Words cannot express how a person arrives at this point—going into hospital and returning home

3

without a baby; having to arrange a funeral for a life that you have only just began to experience. There are no words, no peace, and no hope without knowing that God is a God in the midst of devastation. I am surprised that I was even able to trust in Him and His word. I cried out to God and asked Him to help me deliver a dead baby. I felt his strength. I know that I was able to endure that labor because He was with me.

We had the funeral and the visits. We saw those within our peer group go on to have their babies—healthily and successfully. At that time we were embittered, not because we were sad or discouraged, but because we did not have our own. We had neither the buggy nor the other Christian brothers and sisters surrounding us with cooing and praises. Instead, we had people awkwardly shuffling around us or avoiding us completely. This was probably because they felt unsure or even uncomfortable with our loss. That's often how people feel about loss, especially loss in pregnancy. Words are used more for the comfort of the person sharing them. They are not valuable to the hearer, the person who has just lost the baby, because unfortunately death is final. Barring a miracle, your baby is gone forever.

As a woman, when you see those two lines appear on a pregnancy test, your life changes. Plans that you thought you were making have to be readjusted and sometimes cancelled to make space for this new dependent life that you expect to arrive in about nine months. When this expectation changes or comes to an end, it is not only devastating but requires life adjustments and time to cope with the change.

Church can sometimes be one of the most painful places to be when experiencing such change. Although everyone means well by quoting and sending scripture, the Word for me was so painful to hear in the midst of loss because the enemy (the devil) was having a field day with my mind. I was plagued with questions such as, "With all these promises, why didn't God come through for you?" and "Why didn't God rebuke the devourer? You are a tither." Tempted to dwell on these thoughts, I would tell myself, *Your case was different. You disobeyed, you didn't have enough faith, and you are not as special, anointed, faithful, or blessed as your peers.* The fight became intense.

Three months later, I was pregnant again. The Lord used that time to expose the voice of the enemy and his lies. This revelation would help me greatly in my future losses and pregnancy challenges. Understanding that an Almighty God who has to look after the whole world would come alongside me to teach me the truth of His Word and carry me through my careless speech and bitterness toward new families was mind-blowing and ministers to my heart even whilst I write now.

I gave birth to my two most precious princesses in 2011 and 2013. The first baby was sustained throughout the 40 weeks of pregnancy by the grace of God. The second baby was sustained by the word of God when she came at 26 weeks. Although it may seem that I have skipped the details of these pregnancies, both my children are here because Jesus Christ is Lord. I say this without the intention of using "Christianese" testimonial language. I know that if it wasn't for the power of God, both my children would not be with me now. In the midst of each loss, I was reminded of God's miraculous hand that sustained their lives.

Motherhood took its toll. Having two children who were both under the age of three years old and then embarking on a university degree was not easy. I was completely occupied with managing marriage and looking after my two miracles. This, at times, did not always go as planned, an example being when I found out in September 2016 that I was pregnant. This was right at the start of my third work placement in a civil service organization. This pregnancy was a shock, but secretly I was happy that I was able to conceive again. I felt that no matter what, we would make room in our family for this new child. Not planned but always wanted.

I had a familiar process that I followed after taking a pregnancy test. I would confirm the pregnancy, if possible, with a scan. However, at the scan, it was identified that there was no baby, once again. I had been spotting and the doctors were convinced that this could be another ectopic pregnancy. There were blood tests and more scans but my bleeding increased and still no pregnancy was identified. Heartbroken again but now with family tagging along. Disappointment, sudden hospital trips, mummy very sad and bleeding all the time.

I couldn't understand. Was this spiritual? Was it physical? Or was this just my journey? Why was I unable to have a smooth pregnancy? I had to give this pain over to God as it was beginning to consume me. I have had to learn to give my things to God. This pregnancy was one of those things that I knew I had to hand over. Just like when a child is adamant to do their own shoes up but then begins to struggle to get it done. When a parent steps in and says, "Let me help you," the child realizes that the help would move things along quicker. This was me. I knew that I needed to function—mind, spirit, and body—through this loss. God, as faithful as He always has been, stepped in and took the pain away again. Whilst worshipping Him, I felt it lift from me to Him. Praise Him!!

My last and final loss look place in May 2017. I had decided very early on that I was not going to be afraid during this pregnancy. I recognized that every time that I had to go to the doctors or midwife I would have to share my history. They would ask and I would tell them. Every time I opened my mouth, shame, fear, and embarrassment would flood my heart. The professionals would always want confirmation of my living children. I felt stamped with a sign that said, *"I am unable to carry a baby full term and I need as much help as possible. I am a failure at this thing called pregnancy and I should be extremely 'lucky' (yes, I know it's unchristian to mention luck) to have the living children that I have."* However, I felt this wasn't right. It didn't reflect God's word. God's word told me that I had a fruitful womb and that I would not cast my fruit before its appointed time. God's word said it was His will for humans to go forth and multiply. It also said that I had authority in God's word and I could use my appointed faith to believe for fruitful pregnancy. So I did and I tried as hard as I could to make sure that I was working my best, being there for my family, my church, and not fearing loss. I wanted to just get on with it despite having to attend a pre-term clinic for monitoring and having a surgical cerclage placed at 13 weeks. But then at just 20 weeks, my water broke and though the baby remained alive in me for three days, baby Ira was born at 20 weeks, stillborn.

I believe that the events leading up to this miscarriage and everything happening at this time were truly designed to stop me from believing in Jesus. How could this happen again? How? My pain burrowed into my bones and took up residence. It was compounded by having to explain to two excited sisters that the baby inside mummy had died. I told them that the God they love and trust is watching all this and is in control. However, at the time, I was unsure if God was aware of what was happening. I thought that with this loss, He had left me. It was as if the words that I was holding onto were like sand for me but stone for others. I felt like despite my resolve to trust God in this pregnancy and believe that He would uphold it, He allowed it to end. I have to be honest that I have not yet completely found my place of peace with this last loss. Initially, I felt too much pain and had no response for people who would say, "He allowed it to happen this way," "God is in control," "God will restore," and so on.

At that time, even reading my Bible felt like pouring rubbing alcohol onto a wound. My main question was why He would allow it to happen again. We had suffered before and now again. I recalled the testimonies of people who had endured so much more than we had and were still walking with the Lord. For them, the pain had become a place of remembrance, and not a shrine. I could see in their eyes that they had been with the Lord through their pain and He wasn't afraid of their questions or ugly resentment of their suffering. Instead, He graciously and patiently waited for them to give Him the pain and keep moving.

I think that is where I am now, just moving, giving my pain to God as often as is necessary. I'm allowing forgiveness to flow to those who participated in the events leading to the last miscarriage because that is what Jesus tells me to do. I obey Him because I love Him. I am resting in the knowledge that I have a relationship with God and that He is so aware of 'my ugly' and my management (scatty management) of the bad things that happen in my life. I'm reminded of when I had to deliver Joshua Michael, stillborn. God was not afraid but stayed with me and gave me His strength to get through it.

Now I feel that I know Him more. I understand that although when a loss occurs it feels like He has left the building and taken a flight to Jupiter, God can unravel all the ugly confusion, sadness, pain, anger, grief, disappointment, and doubt and feed us His word at the most perfect time. Only in reflection can you look back and see His hand at work. Now I crave His presence and long to see His word manifest. I also have a stronger desire to pray, especially during suffering.

As I began to write these events down, I felt that I would be able to write chronologically and with a clear flow, but I can't and I don't believe that I ever will be, as these losses have been beautifully entwined by the Lord. He had previously given me the knowledge of His word concerning losing these babies, but now He has also given me an understanding of His covenant love and my relationship with Him. He has shown me that He can handle me and can find me even when I want to reject Him. I can look back and see the times that He has drawn me into His presence and taken away pain that would first make me lose my mind and then destroy my family and finally myself. He has removed the shame associated with multiple pregnancy losses. I don't have a formula but just an encouragement that God, Jesus, and the Holy Spirit are not afraid of our pain or ugliness. So hang on to God. A love like this is worth it even if we don't always get all the answers.

The Anchor Holds: Walking with God in the Midst of a Broken Heart and the Continuing Wait

Heather

My husband Patrick and I have been trying to grow our family for a little over 2½ years. We started trying to conceive about a year into our two-year commitment of serving in a children's home in South India. Our expectation was to come home from our first term overseas as a family of three, but our reality is that we continue to struggle to conceive. In March 2016, we found out we were pregnant, and we could hardly believe it. The ten preceding months of trying and struggling and praying and crying and waiting had culminated in double pink lines on a pregnancy test. The positive result was confirmed with a blood test at the fertility clinic. The news brought lots of celebration and anticipation for God's hand in our lives, meeting us in our desire to have a baby. All of the waiting had been worth it, and we could see God's hand in the timing He had chosen for conception. Our child would have been born around Thanksgiving, and we would have been "home" for the birth of our first baby. This meant getting to share the special moment with our family and closest friends.

Ten days later, on April 1, I started to bleed and we knew that something was wrong. We went to the doctor that afternoon and our fears were confirmed—there was definitely an issue with our pregnancy.

As the hours passed, our doctors began to suspect that the pregnancy was ectopic, so the scene shifted from monitoring me to talking about preparation for surgery. The foreseeable options were for me to take a drug that would cause me to pass the pregnancy or undergo surgery to remove the pregnancy from my fallopian tube. In those moments, Patrick and I were faced with a decision that was too much for us—we knew that we could not make the choice to end the life of a child, even if it might mean harm for me by carrying it out. As tests continued into the afternoon, my husband and I were separated due to the practices in India, which prevent men from being present in the examining room. It felt like we were in an ongoing whirlwind of suspense regarding the outcome of this pregnancy, and we couldn't be together to process it. We started crying out to God to rescue us from our current situation. We began asking for a miracle that God would move the pregnancy into my uterus, or that my body would naturally miscarry the baby on its own. Any other way was too much for us.

Shortly after we began praying like this, my body began to miscarry. Though the outcome was loss, I can tell you honestly that it was in those moments that we experienced the presence and peace of God in a way we will treasure forever. His calm and His with-us-ness were very much evident and we were OK, even in spite of being so alone and so far away from the people who know and love us the most. The doctors He gave us and the way He met us was an inroad to intimacy with Christ and each other that we are actually grateful for.

Our miscarriage was my introduction to grief. Up until that point, although my family had experienced loss, I had never engaged my heart in the process of walking out loss through grieving. This time, I knew I had to, so that I could be healed. What I found is that in the dark days after our miscarriage, as I continued to meet with God through my quiet times, I sensed that He just wanted to sit with me. It was as if He didn't have anything to say; instead, He wanted me to know with assurance that He was in the grief and darkness **with** me. The promise He had given me the day we found out we were pregnant was still true: "I will never [under any circumstances] desert you [nor give you up nor leave you without support, nor will I in any degree leave you helpless], nor will I forsake you or let you down or relax My hold on you [assuredly not]!" (Hebrews 13:5[1]).

God also showed us His kindness and His presence through the experience of others entering into our grief. As we shared about our loss with close friends, God brought people around us who actually grieved **with** us, through tears and words and their presence. He even gave us a precious few who had walked a similar road of loss before us. God brought Psalm 118:7[2] across my path, which says, "The Lord is for me among those who help me." The body of Christ is **beautiful** and our experience of God, through the body, in the midst of our loss, has left us loving the body more, loving Christ more, and wanting to engage, as members of the body, for the sake of others. Our experience was that our loss of the pregnancy was not just ours; it was the body's loss as well.

It wasn't until we were back in the States for a season later that fall and were processing our experiences with some mentors of ours, that I realized one of the core things God did through our miscarriage—deliver me from fear. Their question to me was, "What territory did God give you through that experience?" The verse that came to mind was Psalm 112:7[3], a verse a close friend had sent the day of our miscarriage, and one I had prayed years ago, that He would tattoo on my heart. It says, "He will have no fear of bad news; His heart is steadfast, trusting in the Lord." As I thought on this, I realized that God had met me in what I thought was the worst thing possible that could happen, and He brought me through it! Seeing this actually makes me want to love and trust Him more.

As the months have continued to tick by, some days it feels like our journey with infertility has gotten easier. By God's grace, it's not always looming right there at the front of my mind and heart. Then there are other days when the pain of loss, unmet desires, and the longevity of the road we've been walking is nearly overwhelming. Grief comes with deep mourning for us on those occasions. Sometimes my pain is triggered most when one of those who were walking through infertility and trying to conceive alongside us becomes pregnant. For me, it's like a comrade-in-arms has left the foxhole, and I'm left there. I feel the loneliness, the emptiness, the fear, the questions in my own heart. At those times, I **have** to circle back to promises of Truth that God has given me, or cry out to hear God's voice in the midst of my pain. On one particular occasion like this, the Lord brought a fresh piece of scripture across my lap. Jeremiah 23:23 essentially says (my paraphrase): Am I not a God who is also in the far off (dark, hard, unknown foxholes where you feel so alone...) places?

At another time, God compelled both my husband and me to meditate on scriptures that remind us of God's very specific and powerful work in the lives of so many women who struggled with fertility issues throughout biblical history. It was in the midst of doing this that I sensed the Holy Spirit inviting me to envision those ladies specifically looking on us who struggle—looking on as a "cloud of witnesses," looking on with encouragement to persevere in belief, looking on with an understanding that feels so foreign to most but familiar to them because they have walked it out firsthand and have received the promise, ultimately being in total fulfillment and eternal rest with Christ!

So in the midst of my journey, I am learning that scripture is my fuel for believing in God and continuing in hope because my heart and emotions are so fickle and moved by circumstances I can see. Psalm 27:13-14[4] says, "I would have despaired unless I had believed I would see the goodness of the Lord in the land of the living." His promises provoke me to HOPE—hope that He will, in some way, come through for me in this and somehow make it good. It doesn't mean that we will be able to conceive again, but I do believe we will see God in this, even more than we have already.

Psalm 84:5-7[5] says, "How blessed is the man whose strength is in You, in whose heart are the highways to Zion! Passing through the valley of Baca they make it a spring; the early rain also covers it with blessings. They go from strength to strength, every one of them appears before God in Zion." "Passing through" means this suffering, our loss, is temporary. The "valley of Baca" is a place of weeping. We will **pass through** this valley of weeping. Then it goes on to say that **every one of us** will appear before God in Zion—**We WILL see God!** The road to Zion—to God's presence—includes time spent passing through hard stuff.

In the midst of all of this, what I have found as my resting place is saying "yes" to God, just one day at a time. Rather than trying to fixate on what my story will be or become, I am most at peace when I say, "Today, God, I give you my 'yes'." I'm clinging to Psalm 145:13[6], which says, "The Lord is trustworthy in all He promises and faithful in all He does."

Growing to Desire Life in the Womb

Charlene

I'm a happy mother of a toddler now but, back when I lived in China, I had a miscarriage. It was totally unexpected. My husband and I weren't planning on having a baby, and being a bit advanced in years, I was not looking to get pregnant. I also never had a desire to become one of 'them' (mothers!) whom I considered to be losers with no life other than to be shackled to their children and unable to talk about anything intelligent other than food preparation, material things for the home, and other people's business. Deep down, I did not want to become a mother because I was lacking love from my own mother and I never saw her happy.

One day, my husband and I went to the doctor because I was feeling woozy and weird. I suspected a brain tumor. However, after asking me some questions, the doctor suggested an ultrasound. When the ultrasound technician announced that I was pregnant and we saw the pea-sized being in my womb, I was quite astonished and got, unexpectedly, very excited. It was miraculous to see what was a product of a little bit of both of us and I felt strangely empowered and privileged. Upon hearing that the baby was too small for the stage it was at (the seventh week) and that I was most likely to miscarry, I got overwhelmed with grief and I cried like a baby. The thought of losing this life was so tragic. I wondered if I would meet him/her in the New Heaven and New Earth. Then I fell into a mild depression.

In that 'desert' of a place called Beijing, God sent me support through the few people I knew. My husband was wonderfully supportive and caring. Although he was the one who wanted children, he was non-judgmental and did not blame or interrogate me about what I may have done wrong. He tried to give me a sense of comfort. I also found Sue, my Chinese colleague, to be a Godsend. Her quiet and mature presence was comforting but, oh, her words! She said, "It (meaning the relationship with that particular baby) wasn't meant to be." Normally, I would abhor clichés like this but, somehow, the way she said it helped me accept the fact and gain closure. Sue was a non-Christian presence whom I truly appreciated because she was not giving me pat answers with the over-confidence of some Christians I know who seem to have life and God all figured out. She walked with me, talked with me, and even used a Christian reference for my sake. Although I have since forgotten the reference, I remember being surprised that she would know that and use it to comfort a known Christian. In this manner, God took care of me. He gave me peace and an awareness of His care through people. He enabled me to let go of the feelings of guilt, the regrets, and the what-if's that were bound to drive me crazy.

The wonder of being able to bear life and having nurtured life within me stuck with me. A few years later, when I was about to be in, what my friends considered to be, the very last year to try to get pregnant, I checked with my husband to see what he thought. I wanted a child more for my husband's sake—so that he would be happy and have no regrets. However, he convinced me that it should be 'our' decision because the baby was not going to be just 'his.'

I did not have faith that the baby would turn out 'healthy' or that I would be a good mother. Most of all, I dreaded the criticism and ugly words that I knew my own family members would hurl at me if the baby did not 'turn out well.' Things like, "Why did you wait? You shouldn't have gotten pregnant this late," or "That happened because you are cursed," or "That's the sort of thing that would happen to you!" My husband, however, encouraged me to remember God's goodness and assistance. Even if the baby were born with Down syndrome or some other birth defect, God would give us the love and strength to love him/her and all would be well. It is by the faith of my husband that I was able to take the 'leap of faith.' I am very glad I did.

I cannot explain everything but I do think God redeemed the loss of my first fetus by giving me a sense of wonder for life in the womb and a healthy curiosity and desire for pregnancy. Praise be to God for the life He created and sustained in my womb and which I now hold and behold every day. Our son is truly a masterpiece, a miracle granted unto us.

Finding Answers in God's Love

Amenda

I was 35 years old when I was pregnant for the first time in the October of 2009. The five years prior to that had been a very bumpy course. In the beginning of 2004, my first husband died in a car accident. That was a life-changing point, not only because it truly was from a general point of view, but also because it led to me becoming a Christian. The fundamental change that happened within me caused by the conversion was that I realized that I am not the master of myself or the world around me. I came to see that I belong to the creator and the Savior Jesus Christ. At the end of 2006, I met my husband James and we were married in April 2009.

Regarding having children, James and I both wanted to start a family as soon as possible and we were hoping to have 3-4 children. I was 35 then and felt that there wasn't much time to waste. 2009 was a very eventful year. James and I started going out in January, were engaged in February, got married in Beijing in April and had our blessing ceremony in Oxford in May. In addition to all of this, I quit my job, and we moved to London in August and started our first semester at Bible college in September.

In October, we found out that I was pregnant. At the 12th week ultrasound check in December, we were told that the baby had no life indication and had ceased to grow in the 8th week. It was a shock to us, as we felt the pregnancy was going all right apart from me having had a small urine infection and a bit of a fever and bleeding one day. The contractions and heavy bleeding happened about two weeks after the ultrasound. The time in between was the most painful time because I was waiting for the baby to be delivered. I knew the baby was already gone, but at the same time, he/she was still in my body. That's the most awful experience.

I remember that on our way to the hospital for the ultrasound, James and I, not being aware of the loss of the child, talked about what name we would like to give the child. James randomly (it seemed) mentioned the name "Anastasia," which he explained was a Greek word meaning resurrection. Interestingly, we both thought it was a good and suitable name at that time. We didn't know the gender of the baby and we didn't realize that "Anastasia" is obviously a girl's name. I'm tearful even now thinking about that precious moment. I feel God is talking to me and giving me comfort through the memory of that moment. Now I think the first child God gave us is a girl. We never had the chance to meet our girl in this world but she will be resurrected in Christ and we will meet her one day in heaven.

Once we found out that I was pregnant, we freely told the news to our families and friends. We informed those who were close and also those who were not so close to us. Later on, we realized that this is not common practice. Most people in the UK only announce the news when the pregnancy is beyond the first trimester and the risk of miscarriage is much less. Shortly after the loss, I regretted that we had announced the news so early. There were awkward times when people came to congratulate me about being pregnant and then I had to talk about the miscarriage. However, now I am glad that we told people about the life of the baby from the very beginning. Even though it was a short life, it's still a precious life and is worthy of being celebrated and congratulated.

At the Bible college, which was our community, a lot of the married couples were trying to make the best use of the time at college to have as many children as they could. Children were born one after another. Pregnancy bumps were seen everywhere. It was hard not to covet or to feel resentful during that time. The miscarriage pain wasn't as severe as the pain of childbirth that I experienced years later when giving birth to our son. However, somehow it felt more painful and unbearable.

The hospital that diagnosed the miscarriage recommended we either surgically remove the child or wait for the child to be removed naturally. We didn't want the equipment used for abortions to be used inside my body so we opted to let the child be removed naturally. When the contractions and bleeding came, I went to the toilet. Suddenly I felt that something inside of me was cut off and came out. I didn't look but flushed away the blood. We didn't think much about it at that time. But later on, James and I both felt regret and remorse that we didn't treat our baby's body with more respect. I'm able to get over the feeling of guilt because I trust that all of my weaknesses, shame, and wrongdoings were covered and cleansed by Jesus when He died for me on the cross.

I learned that over fifty surgical abortions happen every minute in China. Many women abort their babies in the early stages of pregnancy without realizing that a lot of the babies would be miscarried later on. That's why we hear about abortion a lot more than miscarriage. In China, the common attitude towards women who have just been through a miscarriage is to blame the woman and assume that there must have been something that she did incorrectly which led to the miscarriage. I experienced that pressure from my parents, which added extra pain and stress.

Looking back, it was a painful journey, but at the same time, it was also a special time of spiritual growth, and God's presence and comfort were very strong and real. When I was struggling and wrestling with questions of why this was allowed to happen, I listened to many of Tim Keller's sermons. All those tough questions found answers in God's amazing love. God suffered the greatest loss of His only son Jesus in order to give me and the child an eternal life.

Two and a half years after the miscarriage, I was pregnant again and gave birth to our son in December 2012. He is a real blessing and a precious gift from God.

A Story of Hope

En Chen

The story of how God put our family together has been full of unexpected miracles and joy, as well as a fair share of challenges and pain. One I wouldn't change for the world, even in light of the recent miscarriage we went through.

We have dealt with infertility for over ten years now, during which we've tried all sorts of treatment from in vitro fertilization (IVF) to Chinese medicine to invasive surgery to you-name-it, we've-tried-it. In that process, we experienced one traumatic ectopic pregnancy and one unidentified pregnancy where they could not locate where the pregnancy was. I really couldn't understand that one. In the midst of failures and heartaches, God also took us on two amazing adoption journeys in China, where we were living, to become a family of four. We had not intended for our lives to unfold this way, but God had a better plan for us. One where we experienced impossible challenges, miracles, and His unwavering faithfulness. In blessing us with our two children, God drew us in and we got to experience Him in a real and intimate way.

Even through these tremendous experiences and blessings, the desire to conceive and have a biological child never left us. Throughout the course of last year, that desire grew once more, possibly fueled by my turning forty. The decision to try one more IVF wasn't an easy one. I struggled through a lot of fear and frustration after having been through so many failures. I was frustrated that even after adopting two beautiful children and experiencing so many blessings, we still have not moved past the ache in our hearts for a biological one. I couldn't understand it and it made me feel helpless. I had a lot of fear about my physical health since I've had my fair share of complications. It was interesting to me that in all our previous attempts, I didn't experience such heavy emotions. This time, however, it was a real challenge. My husband respected my emotions and it really was up to me. The ball was on my side of the court, and I didn't know what to do.

I remember praying to God, asking how I should proceed. On the one hand, I knew our hearts' desire, and on the other, I had such genuine fears and anxieties about it. I remember so vividly God speaking to me over and over, asking me to trust Him. Just proceed. He will protect me. And so we went ahead.

We had decided to try the IVF procedure in the US this time, and that made the project almost a year-long one from decision to final procedures. We had to break up our treatment into three trips. Logistically, coordinating how that was going to happen with our commitments in Beijing and the children's schedule was a momentous task. And each time I was in the US, I struggled both emotionally and physically. The physical pain I experienced was beyond me. And interestingly, I never once struggled this way in all our other IVF attempts. I felt like this time I couldn't rely on my own strength because I had none left. This was the first time I had to fully rely on God to pull me through. I'd cry out to Him whenever the pain and doubts kicked in. And each time, He was there reminding me of His promises, giving me a sense of peace to hold me through.

Then began the dreaded two-week wait to see if we had succeeded. This is the toughest time as your mind races through every scenario and you read into every symptom your body has. The day we were doing the pregnancy test, I remember praying and surrendering to God, giving Him my complete trust that He has the best plan and perfect timing for us. So whatever the result, pregnant or not, I would be at peace with it. But in my heart, I was really preparing for a no. Although I knew full well that if God intended it, it was possible.

So imagine my reaction when we were told, "Yes, you are pregnant." I was so dumbfounded I had to confirm what the nurse said twice. I then broke down and cried. It was from an overwhelming sense of joy, not just about the pregnancy, but the sense that God saw me. He was saying to me, "I see you and I've got this. This time it is different." It was a physical experience I had with God that I will never forget. All the subsequent blood tests and scans were all superb. We got to the six-week scan and even saw all the parts that needed to be there: yolk sac, fetal pole, and heartbeat. I felt a physical sigh of relief as up until then, we were still waiting in anticipation.

Then came the first alarm. After we confirmed the heartbeat, the doctor wanted a repeat scan two days later as the heartbeat was on the faint side. We were told to be "cautiously optimistic." I didn't know what to make of that and believed all was going to be fine. We then began a series of scans and tests, even at different hospitals, to rule out the possibility of faulty machines because our baby wasn't growing as it should. But the heartbeat, though faint, was still there. So we remained hopeful while our doctor gently prepared us for what he thought was the inevitable, a miscarriage. I don't know how we survived the excruciating two weeks of testing every few days. The rollercoaster ride of praying bold prayers and hoping all would be fine, then getting disappointed with the results, then hoping and praying once more. I went on my knees constantly asking God what was happening. How can this be? Did you not say this was going to be different? I could not comprehend what was happening.

Months before we went on this IVF path, we had planned a family and friends vacation on a beach. Once we realized I was pregnant, the plan was for my husband to take my daughter on the trip while I stayed in Beijing with my son. The same day they were meant to leave for the trip, we were due for a test to see if there was any progress. And by then, things really weren't looking good. That morning, I was feeling emotionally spent, and praying for God to show us where this was going. I didn't know how much more of the rollercoaster ride I could take. By then, it had been almost two weeks of uncertainty. I was still hopeful and fully believed that if God intended this to be, He could make miracles happen. However, I also realized that this might not be His answer. It would be impossible for me to comprehend. But I couldn't deny that it was a possibility.

At the doctor's, I immediately saw that the size of the baby had remained small. It even looked as if it had shrunk. And there was no heartbeat. I was numb. I felt a strange sense of relief that OK, at least we know now. We weren't in limbo anymore. After the scan, we had to wait to see the doctor to confirm the results. During the wait, my husband and I were quiet. Then I blurted out, "Am I to stay in Beijing and wait for this impending miscarriage on my own? I can't stay here. I want to leave. Is that even possible?" I realized it might not make any rational sense to want to leave when I had just learned of this bad news but my mind couldn't think of anything else. To me, staying in Beijing to wait for a miscarriage was the worst thing possible. I needed to go to the beach, be with family and friends and process this somewhere else. After confirming the results and consulting with the doctor about the risks of me leaving, we made the decision for me to go. We realized it might have been a risky choice, but it was a risk we took because the alternative was just too painful. I needed to get away.

I packed our bags in two hours, got on the flight, and went to the beach. The trip enabled me to be distracted. I had people around me, I was with the kids, I was busy with activities and immersed in the beauty that was around me. Looking back, I realize God knew exactly what I needed. He gave me the time and space to process what was going on in a beautiful place. A place where I could breathe, a place where I was surrounded by family and friends that love me, and at a pace that I could handle. In that place, there was still crazy laughter and moments of fun. I didn't have to drown in my sorrow or be constantly reminded of the pain I was in. God allowed me to have that time and space. He was that detailed in His love for me.

The first three days things were surreal. I really didn't believe what was happening. I would have moments where I'd talk to God and repeat the same questions. What is happening? I don't understand this. Help me understand. There was silence. In the beginning, my grief and questioning were very polite. I didn't really dare say out loud what was really in my heart. I was still very tentative in how I was making sense of my feelings. There was a lot of rationalizing and repeating of the things I believed. Just trust God. He has a better plan. I can't see it but just trust Him. Really? Am I meant to just take that and move on? The fact was that I didn't understand and I desperately wanted answers from God and He was silent.

After the third day, I broke down and got real with my feelings. It wasn't just that I didn't understand what was happening; it was also a disbelief of how this could be the result. I really questioned God, "What about all the assurances of Your peace and protection throughout the IVF process when I was full of fear and anxiety? What about when I had doubts and You showed me repeatedly that You are a promise-keeping God? What about the affirmation You gave me when we realized we were pregnant? Why put me through all that just to take it away from me? Why would You do that?" Silence.

On top of that, physically nothing was happening and I still had pregnancy symptoms. I tried desperately to make sense of what I was thinking and feeling. Three scenarios began to form in my mind. Scenario one: This ends in a miscarriage and all that God said to me was not true. I must have imagined it all. Scenario two: There is a miracle from God and the pregnancy is somehow saved. All that God said to me holds true. Scenario three: This pregnancy ends in a miscarriage but what God said to me still holds true and was not a figment of my imagination. The third scenario is hard to grasp rationally but maybe there is that possibility because I can't understand how God works. So which one is it, God? Silence.

Now I was finally getting somewhere with my questions. At least I could formulate my thoughts. Scenario one really scared me. If that were true, then what about all the other times I had heard from God, felt His presence and experienced His assurances? Were all of those made up too? If scenario one is true, where does that leave my faith? My faith falls apart. This was really scary to think about but I was questioning and I had to face the realness of it. I believed with all my heart that scenario two was a possibility. I had no doubt that if it was God's will and plan, He could very well perform this miracle and make the baby come back to life. If this was true, we were in for a big surprise. Scenario three felt like a cop-out to me. Isn't this the go-to answer for a lot of things we don't understand in life? God's thoughts and ways are higher than ours. Therefore, who are we to question whether two contradictory scenarios can hold true—all of God's promises are true and yet the pregnancy ends in a miscarriage.

I went back and forth with these three scenarios and couldn't decide which I believed. On top of that, I started to think: What if it was because of something I did wrong or thought wrong? Or was it because I didn't have enough faith and God was punishing me? As I was wrestling with these questions, I spoke to my mum and she reminded me to hold on to the truth of who God is. He is good, He is love, and He does not punish by taking away life. So this did not happen because of what I did or did not do, or because my faith was not strong enough. My Mother made another point that also resonated with me—If we are genuine in our pursuit of Him, if we are sincerely seeking after God and wanting to obey Him, He will not set out to deceive us and lead us down the wrong path. We may not understand the circumstances we are in, but what we do know is that God is good all the time. He is in control and He does not set out to deceive those who are sincerely seeking after Him.

The next day was a beautiful day and we were out on a catamaran. We had gone island hopping and spent the day watching the kids boogie boarding and wave jumping at the beach. It was a full day of adventure and excitement. I remember vividly on the way back, I was out on the deck of the catamaran with my son falling asleep in my arms. All was quiet except for the wind and waves around me. As I looked around surrounded by such beauty, I was suddenly hit by an immense feeling of awe and wonder. The beauty and awesomeness of God's creation was so evident in the sky, water, waves, and shore. I was overwhelmed with a sense of worship and thanksgiving that the God that created the heavens and the earth, this awesome and great God, is the same God that I can call Father. This is the same God that loves me and knows me intimately. The privilege of being His child brought me to tears. In the next moment I was full of questions of why? Why is this happening to me now? As I was feeling the realness of this pain and sorrow, I experienced what it means to be in awe and wonder of God; feeling the intense joy of being His child and at the same time being conscious of suffering and pain. I finally understood what it means to have joy and peace in the midst of our suffering. The joy and peace are in our salvation and hope in our Lord, and no circumstance can change that.

With the holiday over, we returned to Beijing and back to reality. We were due for a doctor's visit because nothing had happened with the miscarriage. At this point, I was really praying for a miracle, that the baby somehow was there with a strong heartbeat. But it seemed that it really wasn't God's intention. The scan still showed the same story. No miracle baby right now. I was immediately faced with having to make decisions about the next steps. On the doctor's advice, we complied with the medication route of inducing the miscarriage. It was a tough decision, as I had wanted to let nature take its course. However, I was still really sick with pregnancy symptoms and I was losing weight.

The next stage of this journey for me was to get through what needed to be done and recover physically. The procedures were horrendous and I really had to rely on God to pull me through. I lost a lot of blood in the process and it took me a long time to recover. Weeks went by. As I was beginning to recover physically, God began to speak to me through worship at church, His words and my daily devotions. It began to be clear to me. All this time, I had been asking God, "Why?" I had been asking for a reason to make sense of what had happened to me. All along there was silence. I realized that God was saying, "I am not asking you to understand, I am asking you to trust me. Can you trust me even when you don't understand?" It sounds incredibly simple but this was a revelation to me. It helped me see that my faith and trust in God had been dependent on me being able to understand. When I didn't understand the circumstances, my faith was shaken. Not understanding made me doubt Him, His promises, His truths, and ultimately His existence! My faith in Him was rooted in what I could predict and understand. I had a map of how life could be, and within that map, I trusted Him. But when He threw a curve ball at me, it shook my faith because that scenario wasn't on my map and I didn't understand it. But isn't the definition of faith to trust in the things unseen? God was now asking me to trust Him even when I don't understand. My faith can't be dependent on my understanding of things. I can't wait for God to answer my whys before I trust Him. That is not faith!

I realized I had a choice to make regarding the three scenarios I had deliberated. I had to choose without understanding the reasons for my circumstances. I chose scenario three: That God is true, His promises to me are real and He is good all the time, even though this pregnancy ended in a miscarriage. An episode to me ended here, but an episode to Him may mean something else. I don't have to understand it but I choose to trust Him and put my faith in Him.

Two months after the medical procedures, my husband and I decided to go away to spend some time together. Just the two of us. It had been a whirlwind of intensity and we needed time away. We spent four days on a beautiful beach watching sunsets, sharing and praying together. On the last night, I experienced the scare of my life. I had a massive bleed that wouldn't stop. We were both in shock and it crossed my mind that this might be it. I may not survive this. We were in the middle of nowhere and how was I to get help? I remembered in the panic I prayed for God to stop the bleeding. And within minutes, the bleeding stopped. Completely stopped. We had the resort doctor check on me and I was given medication to slow down the internal bleeding. The doctor advised us to get help as soon as we got back to Beijing. The next day we made our way home. When the plane landed, I went straight to the hospital. Within two hours, I was in surgery. Apparently, I had continued to bleed internally as the miscarriage was not complete. However, I had had no symptoms in the two months prior to this event. Although we were in shock, the surgery was successful and I was discharged that very night.

Looking back, I realize that God really protected my life throughout the journey. He didn't spare me the intensity of what I had to go through. He didn't make it easy for me at all. But He protected me throughout. I still don't understand why I had to go through this ordeal. But through this, He showed me where my faith was and stretched me to trust Him in the unknown. He encouraged me to trust Him without understanding. Faith is a choice and I have to decide to jump in. He has shown me how it is possible to worship Him in the midst of suffering and have complete joy and peace that He is my Lord and Savior.

I know this journey of desiring a baby is not done. I hold on to His promises that we will conceive and birth a baby. I also trust in God's perfect timing and plan for our family. Until He reveals His plans, I will continue to learn to put my trust and faith in Him no matter what the circumstances are, even if I don't understand. I will also hold on to the truth that He is my good, good Father all the time.

God's Goodness in the Midst of Loss

Charlotte

I miscarried in 2012. Now, that is six years ago. My mum died last year—her cancer spread aggressively with only a few months' notice. I can see now that grieving my baby has grown me to trust that God is good and I can trust him in the more raw and recent grief of losing my mother. It's odd to some, I suppose, that more grief has shown me God's kindness. But in the grief, God has shown up. The certainties I reflected on back in 2012 are no less certain today. I reflected a lot on the things I knew and the things I didn't. The certainties and uncertainties. Why I miscarried: uncertain. Whether God was faithful: certain. Whether God could handle my pain: certain. How He would show that: uncertain.

I felt like I was sitting on a rock. An unmoving rock that was a stable place to yell, cry and ask. The Psalms gave me permission to have unanswered questions, as did Job and Lamentations. Suffering and struggle—even personal struggle, even that which others do not understand or appreciate—is validated in the Bible. He is a God present in the pain. No other religion promises that. God's solution to help a suffering world is to send His Son into it, to be part of it. And take the pain on Himself. So the pain we know now has the hope of an end. We can be raw with God, and His bloodstained Son Jesus is the proof we have hope beyond the aching silence of death.

We had a scan that showed our baby had died. During the next 24 hours, I went through a series of questions. The scan showed that the baby was the size of a six-week, one-day-old embryo. Apparently, after death there can be shrinkage. It may have lived until seven weeks or so. I found myself asking my husband, "What if it never had a heartbeat?" "What if it's just slow to grow and the heart hasn't started beating yet?" "If it had a heartbeat and then stopped, then it died. But maybe it isn't finished yet?" "If it's living, but so undeveloped, what does it look like to die?" I was inconsistent. I knew medical voices would tell me it wasn't yet significant. That it was a scientific process of my body. That is was natural. No, it wasn't!

I wanted to keep being pregnant and I wanted to not be pregnant anymore. Our baby was dead. I wanted to miscarry naturally. I also wanted to stay pregnant and remain physically connected to our baby. We had planned to go on holiday. Now we were unsure about our plans. Having a dead baby inside could lead to a harmful medical situation if it wasn't treated properly. Considering the removal of our baby as a "medical issue" was doctor talk that made me cringe. So impersonal. I had a degree in science but speaking about this deeply personal situation in textbook medical terms was immensely unsatisfying.

I remember the grief of not knowing. Not knowing when our baby died. Not knowing why. Not knowing whether there might have been something I could have done to have a different outcome. All these aspects: uncertain. But God's care in the midst of it: certain. When I first had some spotting on Thursday night it was light and mucus-like. Then nothing until Friday night, when it was more clear mucus with streaks of bright red. Maybe in retrospect like a pre-labor show. Then on Saturday, some more bloodlike spotting. Then on Sunday and Monday, slowly more, not getting to a pad until about Monday, but always more with wiping. And little clots. On Monday, possibly also on Sunday, I definitely had some discomfort around my ovaries. Not much, just a mild ache. Then more bleeding on Monday. I was so tired. I wondered if the sense of discomfort and irritability I felt the night before I went into labor with Number Two was what I was feeling now. Sort of wound up.

Then Tuesday afternoon around 3:30 PM, I started to have contractions. Nowhere like the strength of labor but certainly recognizable as labor. They continued and progressed, quicker and stronger. My sister took Number One home with her and her kids on the train, and it's a very good thing I didn't go with them to the station. I could feel clots and blood passing out onto the pad I was wearing and I started to walk with a waddle. Then I left poor Number Two screaming for me downstairs with a snack and a drink while I disappeared upstairs to try and collect what I was feeling was coming out of me.

I "birthed" our little baby. At first, I thought the baby's pre-body was bound up in a blood clot but as soon as I saw a large, inch-and-a-half by inch sac-like structure, reminiscent of a mini placenta, I stopped looking at the clots. Within a few minutes of this sac coming out the contractions subsided. Although I had never faced this before, I knew that my miscarriage had ended. Strangely, I felt some euphoric sort of feelings in the hours after the "birth." These feelings reminded me of Number Two's birth. I guess it makes sense that the process of miscarriage is the same, physiologically. It's just a lot shorter and less extreme physically, at least for me. I felt quite calm on Tuesday evening, with a strong sense of thankfulness for what God had brought about. I had not needed a D&C, and amidst the discharge, it was very clear what was the beginning of our embryo formation.

I remember contrasting all of my pregnancies and births. I had given birth three times. Three labors. My first two babies went straight onto my belly and began to cry. But this one? My third birth was confronting in its contrast. I birthed it into a recycled ice-cream container with clots of blood. It had no mouth to cry. We put it in the fridge.

I wrote, "*Yesterday (Wednesday) and today, I have found it hard to breathe at times. I have felt like my chest is heavy, as if I am carrying a 2 kg bag of rice on it. Tears are never far below the surface, and I find they tend to come out in waves. Usually they begin with a kind word in a note or a fresh pang of the loss that I feel. Then, I go on to be overwhelmed by the wave. I find it hard to allow those waves in front of the kids. I don't know that they have seen me cry yet. I don't think I'm deliberately holding back but think there are so many things to be done with the kids when I am with them and they are too young to really understand what is going on. I don't want them to think my strong sad emotions are because of them."*

This is a prayer I wrote shortly after our loss:

Dear Lord,

I feel so sad. I want this baby. I want it to be living and growing and its little heart beating. I know you have already given me two babies and may give us more later but right now I am just overwhelmed with sadness. These children are not this child. They are special as are any future children, but they are not this child. This one we hoped for and prayed for, counted days and noted mucus to try for. This one we rejoiced over and anticipated. We told Number One about him. We took photos of Number One, Number Two and a sock monkey with the pregnancy test stick. This was a child we bought a journal for and wrote a letter to. We bought a scrapbook and crafted a page with a space for a photo of this child. The book was to be full of photos showing it growing and living through its first two years. This child will never see this book. I knew it was possible when I bought and implemented these ideas, but it still feels sad that this

has become the reality. So many losses and "will nots."
Number One and Number Two will never hold this baby
and understand that it is their brother or sister. This is so
final. There is no change of status. The baby died and is
dead. We put its developing body in the fridge to keep it
from decaying before the genetic test could happen. We
will get it back tomorrow and need to store it again to
preserve it for Sunday. There are no presents of cute little
clothes to try on, photograph and send to kind friends
and family. There are no "Welcome to the world" cards
to print, no birth notice to draft. I believe that you are in
this pain. I believe you are in this loss and in every detail
of how it has come about. But I just feel so sad right now.

Please use this to help others. Thank you for the reminder
from 2 Corinthians 1:3-5[7]: "Praise be to the God and
Father of our Lord Jesus Christ, the Father of compassion
and the God of all comfort, who comforts us in all our
troubles, so that we can comfort those in any trouble
with the comfort we ourselves receive from God. For just
as we share abundantly in the sufferings of Christ, so
also our comfort abounds through Christ." Amen.

These are some reflections I wrote down about the loss:

"The loss of this baby entails the loss of dreams. The
loss of this life. This loss extends beyond me and our
family—this baby would not be a cousin at that age.
Friends and family surrounding me are impacted by our
loss and our grief. Their own questions are precipitated
by our loss. I keep thinking about desires, and there are
many in thinking about this pregnancy and baby... now
these desires still remain but they are not, cannot, will

not be granted in this baby, in this time. The general ones may yet be—to have another child, give a live sibling to Number One and Number Two, be pregnant while our housemate is also pregnant... but the specifics... giving birth within a fortnight of my housemate, those babies growing up with a shared knowledge of their special history...gestated together in the house...Her Number One and my Number One sharing in having pregnant mummies together without confusion of different due dates...no. These desires cannot be met.

"*Because it is fresh in my mind, I am very aware that these desires are directed at God. I believe that He has ended this pregnancy but I know that He is good and loves me. I am conscious of not wanting these desires to become demands of God, which would, I think, lead me to feel angry that God has done this to me. But I am so thankful that for now, this is not what I see. I do not feel this anger. I am just thankful for what we have had and for so many things about how the end has come. I am not without hope or peace. We are all in God's hands, not just our little baby. I have been reminded time and time again of God's sovereign work and goodness through this pregnancy and its end.*

"*When talking about the baby that was lost, I want to say 'he' or 'she,' not 'it'. To say 'he' or 'she' reminds me and the world that this was—albeit right at the beginning of—a little human's life. Although there is neither male nor female in Christ, there is something profound about gender reflecting the image of God and it reflects God's perfect design. To talk of 'it' separates our baby from this creation somehow, even if just linguistically. But given*

linguistics is one of the few tools we have to mark and
remember, I want to use it all we can."

It was so strange to be seen by the world and yet no one could see what had happened unless they knew it because I had told them. Grief was real, even if other grief at later stages of pregnancy was bigger or more poignant. I felt angry when awkward friends suggested that because I already had two children this was not a great loss. No! This loss did not need to be undermined or qualified. The young age of my baby made it no less significant in our family life. The fact that I was clearly fertile and could probably try for another baby later did not comfort me in the pain of losing *this baby*. Was the need for others to reduce the pain for me more about their comfort interacting with me, or about genuine desire to bring me comfort?

I was afraid of silence. The silence when the phone messages stopped and the emails ceased. The world assuming I was OK, or should be OK. I feared getting angry at the invalidation of grief—feeling a need to justify why it was OK to be sad for as long as I was sad. Actually, the overwhelming response was validation. Almost complete understanding that this was hard for us as a family. Of course, the external messages of support died down. We in the West do not do well at remembering the waves and seasons of grief that can come later—on significant dates...at milestone ages. But God is a constant confidant to share this grief with, whether or not the world knows.

I spoke to a woman at my Bible study two days after miscarrying. She had had two or possibly three miscarriages, one so early it was hard to tell. Years on, with adult children, she still wonders about what her other children would have been like. The grief of her own loss could come, even then, in waves, especially when she heard of someone else facing a similar thing. I guess I wondered if people who hadn't faced this themselves could understand the ongoing nature of grief...silent, through all sorts of life events. Rarely voiced, because we don't like to speak about such things very often. The woman said that she had one miscarriage between her two boys. Her third pregnancy was very soon afterwards. So if she had had the second child she wouldn't have had Number Three. She said she wasn't quite sure what to think about that. I reflected on what she said. Ultimately, God's sovereignty and kindness must make sense of it, even if we cannot synthesize it clearly.

When I began to bleed, I had a very strong realization that God is the sustainer of life and the baby's life was only continuing (if it was, which I discovered later it was not) under His care. Then I began to think about how much of a blessing it was to reflect on this. Through my two earlier uneventful pregnancies, I paid lip service to God's miraculous work in sustaining life. Now, I know it deeply with a fresh angle. God had sustained their fragile lives and still did at 1½ and 2½. I'm not sure I felt the rug had been pulled out from under me. I never particularly thought I would miscarry, and hadn't worried about telling people we were pregnant quite early on. I figured if we did miscarry I would prefer people to know, and if we didn't it would be fine for them to have already heard.

My early thoughts were that God is good, all the time, and in this, even if I didn't want this outcome, He was still good. He must have some way of bringing His goodness to bear in all that. Someone commented to me shortly afterwards that they were encouraged I seemed so thankful in this and that it seemed to have pushed me towards faith, not away from it. I said that I could see years of Bible teaching, studies, learning and growing had piled up and shaped my head, which was now in turn shaping my heart response. I never thought at the time that it would be those multiple years that would cumulatively give me a picture of God and suffering to undergird this season with such foundation. I'm so thankful for the countless people God has given over many years to put those bricks in place. I didn't see that as me being full of faith. I think God is gracious and has done that shaping and has put those people there. If I knew God's character, if I knew the beauty of Jesus, why would I go anywhere else?

Since we lost that little one, we discovered that he was a "he." And he—Thomas Mikononi ("Mikononi" means "in God's hands")—had a genetic condition that meant he could not be born alive. Perhaps one angle of God's kindness to us was saving us from the grief that would have eventuated if I had carried him for longer. Perhaps what we learned in that season was sufficient for that season. In our good Father's hands, since that time we have found that life is no less complex or easy. In fact, the grief has got deeper and harder. But the paradox is that in the deeper grief, God's gentleness has deepened further.

"We know the pain reminds this heart that this is not our home...
What if the greatest disappointments, and the achings of this
life is the revealing of a greater thirst this world can't satisfy?
What if trials of this life are your mercies in disguise?"
—Laura Story

Where Hope and Healing Are

Sarah

My miscarriage occurred in August 2012 when I was a new immigrant to Canada, about two weeks before I got my free medical care. I had spotted for about 10 days before I realized something might be wrong. Somehow, my first guess was that I could be pregnant. The test turned out positive! It was such a surprise! My husband was so proud of becoming a Daddy. We had high hopes for the baby, whose name was John. I just knew it was a boy. I started to dream about our new life. A few months later, we were supposed to return to China, where I'm from but I loved Canada and wanted to stay. I hoped that with the coming of our first child my husband would change his mind and settle down in Canada.

All of a sudden, life seemed full of exciting possibilities. However, when I called my mother she said she was concerned about the spotting and the mild cramps. She told me I might have had a threatened miscarriage and I needed medical attention and possibly bed rest. Bed rest? What was that? Miscarriage? Impossible! We looked on the Internet and it seemed many ladies spotted and had cramps during their pregnancy. My optimistic husband suggested that I wait and see since there were only two weeks remaining until I would obtain my free medical care. It sounded reasonable. Life went on. My cramps became heavier and I was spotting more. My mother kept calling me and asking me to get medical attention, while my husband reminded me it would cost a lot to see a doctor in North America and we only had about a week to wait.

It was difficult waiting. I prayed a lot. I prayed that God would keep my baby and me safe. I didn't just have the baby to worry about. I also feared the occurrence of another stroke. I had had a stroke in May, a month before coming to Canada. Doctors ran every test but couldn't find the cause of it. The discovery that I was pregnant gave me hope. I thought it would be too cruel for God to allow me to have another stroke while being pregnant. God must have given me the baby to reassure me that I was healed and there would be no more strokes.

However, each new cramp, each new spotting was like a hammer knocking on my heart, attempting to break my hope and even my faith in God's power and mercy. One beautiful afternoon, I went to a nearby beach alone (not quite alone since my baby was with me). It was a rocky beach and the ground was nicely toasted by the sun. Another wave of cramps came. I sat down, feeling the baby. It was painful. I described to my baby how pleasant the surroundings were and I told him that everything was going to be OK for God had made him and would take care of him. The wind smelled salty. It felt like the baby and I were so connected. I loved him, with such tender, motherly love. That afternoon, there were two people at the beach, my baby and me.

When the spotting turned into light bleeding, I realized that the baby's life could be in jeopardy. There were only a few days before medical care became free for me but I could wait no longer. My husband and I went to see the doctor, who was supposed to arrange a meeting with a specialist the next day. The next day, I passed a big blood clot and the severe pain in my lower abdomen struck me down to the bathroom floor. I had a feeling that the blood clot could be the baby, but I wouldn't believe it. The cramps were so heavy that I couldn't get up and make it to the car. My husband panicked and called the ambulance. Lying on the cold tile floor, again and again I prayed that my Heavenly Father would keep the baby. I told my baby that Mommy wouldn't let him go. His maker would protect him. The heavy cramps were nothing like what I had ever experienced and it felt like the ambulance was never coming. Overwhelmed by the pain, I told God that if it were his will he could take the baby away.

In the emergency room of the hospital, the ultrasound test showed that there was nothing in my uterus. Though I was prepared, I was still disappointed. According to my blood work, I was only about five weeks pregnant, not six or seven weeks as I thought. The doctor said some babies, due to natural selection, just wouldn't make it. I quietly accepted what he had to say. He was surprised by "how well I handled it."

I took the news quite well. It was late at night when I was released from the hospital. My husband was in such a hurry to go home that I had to run after him to the car. It was hard to run right after a miscarriage, but I did it anyway. It was hard to have a miscarriage, but I had it anyway. I didn't have a baby with me anymore. My baby was flushed down the toilet. How did he die? Did he not have enough nutrition so he starved to death? Did he not have enough oxygen so he suffocated to death? I didn't know how to grieve for my baby. I didn't think it would be normal to grieve for a three-week-old fetus, so I shed a few secret tears and acted strong.

I believed that God took my baby away. His name was John. He was going to travel the world spreading God's good news to the people. Now I don't have him anymore. Would I have another stroke? It would be too cruel for me to have a stroke while I was pregnant but now I was not pregnant anymore. We were going back to China. I tried to use the coming of the baby to persuade my husband to change our plan and settle in Canada (the dreamland to many Chinese) but the baby was gone and the dream was broken.

The next Sunday, during worship, God spoke to me through the lyrics of the songs we sang. "There may be pain in the night, but joy comes in the morning. My hope is Jesus and nothing else." I gave thanks for God's promising words and realized that I had built my hopes on the baby, rather than the Lord. I even tried to force my husband to change his plan with the excuse of the baby. The message was uplifting, but somehow I interpreted it this way—the baby had become my idol so God had to take him away to correct me. In my heart, God, the gracious, tenderhearted, and patient Father, turned into a scary, vengeful old man standing behind me with a big rod in his hand.

I had only been a Christian for two years then. God had been very kind to me. He answered my prayers, talked to me from the Bible in miraculous ways, and healed my sickness many times. I thought I loved him dearly until he took my baby away. I knew that God could do anything and that his ways are mysterious. Deep down in my heart I felt betrayed, but I buried my bitter feelings and moved on.

I wanted a baby so badly. There was a big empty hole in my heart that I needed a new baby to fill. Four months after my miscarriage I was pregnant again. This time, I was ready to fight for the baby. At the first sight of spotting, when I was around six weeks pregnant, I went to the doctor. It turned out that my progesterone levels were very low. I had injections, took pills and went on bed rest until the 10th week. Our daughter was born strong and well. Praise the Lord!

It seemed like everything went on well, but not quite. After the miscarriage, I didn't share my feelings with anyone successfully. I tried to talk to my husband, but the conversation didn't really go very far. He didn't understand. In fact, I didn't even know what I wanted to share. I used to be carefree and easygoing but then I became intense, defensive, and fearful. I changed.

After the miscarriage, I suffered from depression and anxiety disorders for almost three years. The symptoms were almost unnoticeable at first, but as they got worse, I realized that I needed help. I prayed a lot during those years. I prayed that the Lord would take my fears and anxiety away. God answered my prayers. Once, after a church service, I heard a loving whisper in my heart, "I just want to be your friend." But back then, I was so troubled that I couldn't respond to God's offer of friendship.

Later, I realized that I was actually very angry with my husband because I thought it was his cheapness that cost me the baby. He discouraged me from seeing the doctor for financial reasons. If he had supported me to get blood work done, we might have been able to find out that it could be my low progesterone levels that caused me to miscarry, not that the baby had a defect, as the doctor had said. Deep down, I was filled with anger, but I knew reconciliation was necessary. One Sunday, after hearing a sermon on forgiveness, I brought up the issue. My husband, a very reserved man, finally shared the feelings and concerns he had during and after the tragedy. He wasn't cheap. He didn't know how serious it could get. He was young, ignorant and helpless, just like I was. He said he was very sorry. I forgave him, quick and easy! We talked a lot that night and apologized to each other for many other things we had done wrong to one another. It was a turning point in our suffering relationship.

I thought I would get better then, but I was still anxious and full of fear. A few months later, our pastor preached another message on forgiveness. I came to an awakening: I was angry with God about my miscarriage and I needed to reconcile with Him too. I repented for holding bitterness, a grudge and distrustfulness against God. Surprisingly, I was relieved. I was over all of the trauma. I was set free. I was healed. All praises to the gracious King!

Romans 8:28[8] says, "And we know that all things work together for good to those who love God, to those who are called according to His purpose." In my anguish, I could not see what good it could bring to lose a baby. "I was once blind, but now I see." I had heard of God's gentleness and friendship but now I'm sure of them. God had been with me throughout all the torment. Although, for a long time I couldn't feel His presence and couldn't love Him back, His healing hands were always outstretched towards me. He brought me many people who genuinely cared about me. I often felt loved and encouraged.

I've learned to build my hope on God, not on worldly passions. "Trust in the LORD with all your heart and lean not on your own understanding" (Proverbs 3:5[9]). "For I know the thoughts that I think toward you, said the LORD, thoughts of peace, and not of evil, to give you an expected end" (Jeremiah 29:11[10]). I am now able to sympathize with women who have lost their babies, from either miscarriage or abortion. Like many people in China, I did not consider a fetus to be a life. Actually, I had never pondered over the meaning and value of human life before I lost my baby. A friend of mine told me that before she aborted her first baby, she struggled. She felt the great mother's love for her baby, not a fetus, her baby. It was hard to let go of it. I felt the same. I was very ready when God called me into the pro-life ministry in China.

Since I was delivered from depression and anxiety, God had brought several people suffering from the same problems into my life. I helped to counsel them and one of them is now set free. Hallelujah!

I don't know why I had a miscarriage but I do know that I didn't really lose my baby. Although his time on earth was short, he has eternity with God. God made him and God is faithful. I will see him in heaven one day.

"Do not be anxious about anything, but in every situation, by prayer and petition, with thanksgiving, present your requests to God."
(Philippians 4:6[11])

Pure Joy

Rachel

After an initial greeting, James opens his epistle with the following, "Consider it pure joy, my brothers and sisters, when you face trials of many kinds…" (James 1:2[12]). A long time ago, I heard a sermon about this verse in which my pastor emphasized the first word: consider. A trial is, at the very least, painful. The degree of pain could range from mild to excruciating to absolutely unbearable. Joy is not on the spectrum of natural responses to any trial. Instead, we have to *consider* it pure joy when we face trials. Why should something painful be considered pure joy? James goes on to say, "Because you know that the testing of your faith produces perseverance. Let perseverance finish its work so that you may be mature and complete, not lacking anything" (James 1:3-4[13]). Painful trials are one of the ways God chooses to strengthen us in our faith, to mold and form us more and more into the image of Christ.

Before I had children, I always thought that miscarriage would be a trial I simply could not endure. How horrible it would be to know a life was growing inside you and then was no more. How painful it would be to have this hope of life, this expectation to bring a little one into the world and then be left with nothing. Little did I know that miscarriage was one of the fiery trials that God would lead me through.

I was more than surprised when I found out I was pregnant. I was approaching forty, already had five children, was running 35+ miles a week, and was still breastfeeding my toddler. Honestly, I thought menopause was just around the corner. Apparently, I was wrong…menopause was not on the horizon. A new baby was. My husband was delighted. My kids were so excited that they threw a surprise baby shower for me. I had a little bit of back pain here and there but otherwise I felt like a normal pregnant mother of five. I saw the heartbeat at my seven-week ultrasound and it seemed like everything was progressing normally. I decided not to have a twelve-week checkup, since the midwives gave me the option. Instead, my next checkup was somewhere between fourteen and fifteen weeks. Since I saw the heartbeat though and had no indication anything was wrong with the baby growing inside me, we announced to the world via Facebook that we were having a sixth child! We were full of joy and were already thinking about how we would arrange the bedrooms to accommodate the new addition. There was never even an inkling that something would go wrong.

I took my girls along with me to see the midwife for my routine checkup. They love coming because the midwife usually allows them to help out with the Doppler. The midwife pulled out the Doppler and spent a long time searching for the baby's heartbeat. Eventually, she hooked up their antiquated ultrasound machine and found the baby. She did see a flicker indicating a heartbeat but was very concerned that the baby didn't seem to be moving at all. She escorted the girls to the waiting area and discussed with me her concerns that this baby may not have survived. To further evaluate the situation, she ordered an ultrasound to be performed at an imaging center. The ultrasound revealed the baby was still alive but not doing well. The baby's heartbeat was only sixty beats per minute, far below the normal range for the baby's gestational age. The baby was also measuring closer to twelve weeks, three weeks smaller than indicated by my due date. Nonetheless, I still had hope. I continued praying. I asked my small group to pray. I believed with all my heart that God could sustain the life of my unborn child.

Since nothing dramatic (like cramping or bleeding) happened over the weekend, we followed up with another ultrasound, at which point the ultrasound detected no heartbeat. After fifteen weeks, our baby was no more. I maintained composure at the imaging center before all the apologetic staff assuring them that I have five beautiful, healthy children. But, the moment I got to the sanctuary of my car, the tears began to stream down my face. *Why, God, why? You know I am not strong enough to handle this.* Then, my thoughts turned away from God and to myself. *Surely, I did something wrong to cause this to happen.* I began to evaluate every move I had made over the past three months.

> Why did I continue to run so much?
> Why didn't I drink more water?
> Why did I drink so much tea?
> Why did I dig out those bushes?
> Why did I sit in the hot tub for that one minute?
> Why didn't I eat more and more often?
> Why did I carry Josiah around so much?
> Why didn't I stop nursing Josiah?

Then, my thoughts moved from the physical to the mental realm. Maybe I was ungrateful for a sixth child. Maybe the opinions of those around me, who already thought we had more than our share of children, had started to affect me. Maybe God thinks I'm a horrible mommy and doesn't want me to have any more children. Maybe I'm doing enough damage to those I have. I longed to have some reason to explain what happened, I suppose, so that I could make sure it would never happen again.

I conducted a little bit of research and discovered that oftentimes miscarriages are the result of chromosomal abnormalities present at the time of conception. These abnormalities cause either the mom's body to stop supporting the baby or the baby's body to just shut down. This set me free from the guilt I had been inflicting on myself. I no longer believed that I had done something to harm the life of my child. I no longer felt that I was to blame for this tragedy.

However, one question remained unanswered. Why? Why did God allow this to happen to us? At the time, we had been studying the life of Joseph in our family devotions. So many *bad* things happened to Joseph. His brothers sold him into slavery and reported him as dead to their father. He was falsely accused of rape and thrown into prison. He helped others in prison but was forgotten by them. Yet, Joseph humbly accepted every situation and continued to trust in God. In the end, Joseph tells his brothers, "You intended to harm me, but God intended it for good to accomplish what is now being done, the saving of many lives" (Genesis 50:20[14]). At the end, Joseph could see the *good* that God had brought out of the *bad* and how God was glorified through those trials. I had to make a conscious choice to be like Joseph. I had to consider the trial pure joy. I had to stop focusing on what was at that point unknown and focus on what was known. What was known to me then is still known to me now. God, my heavenly Father, is loving and wise and good. Everything that He allows me to go through, whether good or bad, is both for my good and His glory. He has promised never to leave me and He is with me every step of the way. In fact, He carries me every step of the way.

Our church was very supportive of us during that time. Friends offered to bring meals and to help out with our children. I think everyone grieves differently, though. Such offers touched my heart and showed me that people cared, but I felt that if I took everyone up on their kind offers, it would have delayed the grieving process for me. I found it helped me to resume normal life, to spend time serving my husband and my children in the home. I busied myself with cooking, cleaning, and schooling. Nonetheless, the grieving process takes time. It was hard going to church that Sunday. I still looked pregnant, but I wasn't and that felt strange. Oddly, the first person to talk to me that day was one of our deacons. I had never had a conversation with him before. He is a big, burly guy and was single at the time, not the type you would expect to show compassion to a woman struggling with the loss of a baby. He made a point to come over and sit with my husband

and me before the service began and tell us that he had been praying for us. After our brief conversation, he sent me a link to an article assuring me from the Scriptures that unborn children are ushered into the very presence of God. This meant so much to me and continues to be a memory I treasure in my heart.

As I meditated on the death of our unborn child, my heart rejoiced at knowing that our child went to be with the Lord. It is wonderful to think of him or her being with God in heaven, a place free of sin and pain and death. The more I thought about our child in heaven, though, this joyfulness was intermingled with sadness. My hopes of worshiping God together with my child were dashed as I contemplated what little I knew about our child. The baby didn't live long enough for us to find out if it was a boy or a girl. The only glimpses that we saw were the ultrasound images, which more closely resembled an alien than an actual human being. We never got to hold our baby and gaze into its eyes or comb its hair. We don't know if it would have had blue or green eyes, red or blonde hair. There was no special feature that I could use to distinguish my child from any others in heaven. How would I ever recognize my child? I struggled and struggled with this question in my thoughts, too embarrassed to actually express my concerns to anyone lest they really see how small and weak my faith really was. One day, I lay in bed crying and crying and praying silently, when my husband came in and asked me why I was crying (and why I wasn't tending to our children). At that point, I was so desperate for an answer that I just blurted everything out between wails. David was very gentle with me and didn't rebuke me for my lack of faith, but simply asked, "Who is our child with right now?" OK, I knew the answer to that one, "Well, God." "And God knows all things, right? (rhetorical question...He didn't even give me the opportunity to answer!) "God is going to make sure you know your child. You *will* be able to worship God together!" My husband was the Lord's messenger to me that day bringing me great comfort and assurance.

After that day, I thought I had completely dealt with the grief of losing my child. Every question was resolved. Yet months later, I sat in church and witnessed a baby dedication. When I should have been rejoicing with the other parents, feelings of intense sadness suddenly rose up from within. I ran out of the church with tears streaming down my face once again, just as they had months earlier. If my baby had lived, I would have been standing in front of the church body alongside the other parents dedicating my child to the Lord. But, I wasn't there because my baby did not live. Again, I had to remind myself to *consider* it pure joy because God was using this to draw me closer to Him, to change me more and more into His image.

From where I stand now, I can see how God used this trial to strengthen my faith in Him. I found that I could not handle the trial of a miscarriage and perhaps that was part of the point. I was only able to go through it by relying on Him and His grace, by meditating on the truth of His word, and drawing close to Him in prayer. God has also used my struggle to comfort and support others going through similar trials.

Since then, God has been gracious enough to grant us yet another child, a beautiful girl, named Chaeli Lynne.

A Momentary Bitterness

Naomi

"You should really take care of your body. You might not notice it now, but when you're older you'll regret it." "Thank you, but I think now is not the time to talk about that," I responded with a forced smile. It's the kind of smile I use when I want to soften my bluntness but I don't know how to soften the words, so I smile with my lips pursed instead.

He fell silent, which was so unusual for him. He always had a story to share to explain his point. With sincere concern, he had come with his wife to visit us, but he suddenly realized the failure of his attempt to comfort. Still, his attempt was better than the nurses', who told me I was young, that I could have another, that I already had two children.

His attempt was much better than the operating room nurse who didn't even know that I was having a stillbirth instead of an abortion. She felt so awkward when I began to cry. I was not loving in my response. I told her that since she was not a mother and had never wanted and lost a child, she could not understand my pain. Do not tell me not to cry. Indignant, I wanted to tell her how getting pregnant with one is one thing, but did she understand how rare it was to get pregnant again with twins? Did she understand how I initially didn't want to be pregnant at all, but then rejoiced when I learned how special this pregnancy was, only for it to be ripped away from me? But my language skills thankfully failed me, and God graciously did not loosen my lips so I could stumble in sin.

My husband, Bobby, walked our friend and his wife out, and they asked to pray for him one more time after praying over me. "He said you were much stronger than his wife had been," Bobby said when he came back. "He said that she was hysterical, and that I should really take care of you." He took my hand in his. "Was I wrong to tell him it wasn't an appropriate time to talk about his views on traditional Chinese medicine? Did I say that OK?" I looked him in the eyes. "I think how you said that was great," he ran his hands through my hair and kissed my cheek.

I felt like a prisoner in my hospital bed, forced to stare at the tacky hospital decor that was meant to seem like a palace. I wanted to run. I wanted to scream. But on the outside, I mostly only showed a calm and cool demeanor until I was put to the test. The next day, I had a temper tantrum and made one of the hospital's doctors so mad or so upset that she started to cry. I screamed. I was outraged that they weren't going to allow Bobby in the room with me during one of the procedures. Was this not an international hospital? Why weren't they acting international? Bobby was shocked at how I acted and grieved, but he understood. I didn't want to be away from him.

With so many assailing comments and phrases that I understood in this language, I couldn't avoid the careless darts. I couldn't avoid it like the other expats who don't understand a single drop of the language. I didn't want to hear how the medical staff gossiped about my situation or offered advice, but I couldn't tune them out. I just wanted to hold Bobby's hand and cry and pray. I wanted to be hidden and covered and not face this trial.

Then, in the midst of all of this culture shock, our local church family came to visit. All of the brothers who came were so somber while the sisters had clearly been crying before they even came into the room. They understood. They knew the preciousness of life and that it wasn't to just be tossed around so carelessly. They had wanted these twins for me as much as I wanted them.

A brother who was five years older than me began to weep. He lived with our family and he would often cook, as it was his hobby. "I'm so sorry I didn't take care of you more. I thought you were so strong, and now this has all happened..." His regret was clear, but we assured him that God gives and takes away, and God is good in all circumstances. The rest of the family sat with us in silence. They prayed over us, and one sister came and hugged me, weeping with me. Throughout the next month these brothers and sisters would help take care of our whole family physically, providing childcare and food when we needed it. They understood our hearts, and their love helped soothe the wounds of words created by a godless culture. One sister told me later, "The other locals just don't know what to say. They don't have the hope that we do. We don't talk about these kinds of things in our culture; we just stuff it down. We speak of it in whispers."

The last day of the hospital stay, when I had to actually give birth to my lifeless twins, Bobby and I spent the day alone. Together we went to the delivery room. Together through the pain of the pushing and contractions, he and I quoted scripture to help my mind focus on hope rather than despair. Bobby said watching me bear this was the most painful experience he has ever had in our marriage. Oddly, what has been hardest for me has not been the actual event of the stillbirth, but the aftermath.

I am so ashamed of how I acted in those moments of weakness, that in the midst of trial I didn't respond with love. I can't say with confidence that the labor and delivery nurse who asked about us quoting scripture wants to learn more about God because of our testimony to her. At the time, she said she was surprised we were so strong, but how can she not remember how I was screaming in anger at the doctor in my room? And I can't say with confidence that I have rejoiced in God's goodness at every moment. No. I've questioned it. Why on earth did He allow this to happen?

I also often wade through questions of "what if?" What if I had cared for my health better? What if I had relaxed more? What if I deserved to lose them? What if God took them away from me because I haven't stewarded my relationships well with my first two children?

And in these bitter moments when no one else is aware that a pain still brews in my heart like a coffee pot mistakenly left on—where the coffee sits and warms and cakes and then the brown stains are impossible to wash out completely—in these bitter moments God has been close to me.

It was a grace to learn that they were boys. We named them Perez and Zerah after Judah's twins. Providentially I had been gifted a set of twin boys onesies, and I keep these tucked away. When I need to grieve over lost dreams of giggles and baths and kissing toes, I pull them out and cry. I also put on a very special playlist when I need to grieve. The songs are full of scripture and reminders that death is a part of life. And it's painful. Jesus never promised me a beautiful, painless life when I followed him. On the contrary, following him was always meant to be hard. But he gives this meaningless life of death so much purpose with his promise of eternal inheritance.

That playlist is full of songs that remind me of this truth, "So we do not lose heart. Though our outer self is wasting away, our inner self is being renewed day by day. For this light and momentary affliction is preparing for us an eternal weight of glory beyond all comparison, as we look not to the things that are seen but to the things that are unseen. For the things that are seen are transient, but the things that are unseen are eternal" (2 Corinthians 4:16-18[15]).

And when I look past that I've lost twins on earth, I see that I've gained children waiting for me in heaven. They have already obtained what my heart hopes for, an eternity with my love, my savior. And certainly, God does continue to use my pain to reach out to a desperate world. The women here who don't talk about their miscarriages and stillbirths, who just stuff down the emotions as they're supposed to. They have no one who can offer them a glimmer of hope or truth.

I have confidence that it's OK to cry. It's OK to hate death. Even Jesus responded to death with tears. He would have cried with me, just like He cried for Lazarus. Just like He called out on the cross. Bearing a painful moment doesn't have to be met with only smiles and joy, though I have hope He will turn my suffering to laughter and wipe away my tears.

And on that day, receiving my heart's desire, I will consider all of this momentary pain to be worth it.

Little Princes

Ariel King

On October 5, 2014, our family got the biggest surprise of our lives. Almost eight months after giving birth to our first daughter, we found out we were expecting again. My husband, Derek, and I met in the cafeteria of our junior high school in 2008. I will never forget his first words to me: "I'm going to marry you one day." Aside from the fact that I had no idea who this guy was, how could I not think he was crazy for thinking of marrying ANYONE at the age of fourteen? Little did I know that God would take that silly eighth grade boy and mold him into the husband and father who works hard to provide for our family day in and day out.

Our plan, like many others, was to wait until we were married to start a family. Unfortunately, we gave in to temptation and conceived our first child the week of our high school graduation. Two months later, July 26, 2013, we went to the courthouse and were joined as husband and wife.

My first pregnancy went by fairly easily with minimal complications. I experienced the normal pregnancy symptoms we always hear about (morning sickness, cravings, discomfort) and also plenty that aren't really publicized, such as round ligament pain and preterm labor. I was put on bed rest at 28 weeks gestation just as a precaution. On February 12 2014, twelve days before my due date, I gave birth to a beautiful baby girl. She had us hook, line, and sinker. We had always talked about one day having more children, but we planned to wait until our first baby was, at the very least, out of diapers. After I gave birth, I began looking into birth control options, while also praying and turning to my Bible for help. Ultimately, we felt led to forego all contraception and leave the growth of our family in God's hands.

Fast forward to the night we found out we were pregnant again: we were THRILLED to be parents once more. Sure, we were scared. I mean, we never expected to get pregnant so soon after our first, but we knew this baby was meant to be here. At the time, we were living with some family members, so we immediately starting making plans to get our own place. Next came our baby plans. The room. The crib. The name. We wasted no time falling head over heels in love with this unexpected blessing.

Our excitement grew and grew, almost as fast as my bump! At seven weeks pregnant, I couldn't believe how much I was showing; we began to suspect twins (which only made our excitement stronger)! After weeks and weeks of going back and forth with my insurance company, we FINALLY got an appointment to go and see our little monkey(s) on November 14!!!! But neither of us expected what came next...

We arrived at the hospital thinking that we were about to see our sweet baby twisting and turning. That we would get to hear his/her heartbeat galloping strong. We walked into the sonogram room, the tech squeezed the warm jelly on my stomach, and we watched and waited. This sonogram was unlike any of the ones I experienced with our oldest. The tech was quiet. I began to worry. I started to ask if something was wrong. She didn't look at me. She didn't answer. I started to panic. I could feel in my bones that something wasn't right. She finally spoke, "I'll be back in a few minutes," and walked out. After what seemed like a lifetime, she came back in to give us the news that would change me forever.

"The sonogram shows two babies. But we can't find the heartbeats," she said. "It seems that one baby stopped growing at around five weeks' gestation, and the other at around seven weeks. Both sacs stopped growing on or around the 21st of last month. I'll give you a few minutes if you need it." I couldn't believe what I was hearing. I couldn't breathe. I couldn't speak. I broke down.

How could this happen? Why me? Why us? What did I do wrong? How could my body betray me? What did we do to deserve this? Am I being punished? What will everyone think? What will they say? HOW will we even tell them?

My mind just wouldn't stop. We had already announced our pregnancy. We told everyone that we were going to see our baby that day. I knew that the texts, phone calls, and messages would start rolling in at any time asking how the appointment went. I couldn't face it. And yet it didn't seem real...until I HAD to tell someone. I was on the schedule to work that afternoon but there was NO way that I could go to work in that state of mind. I called my manager and told him why I couldn't make it, and it hit me ten times harder.

My OB-GYN called and scheduled a follow-up for the next week. They said that I may not have been far enough along to see the heartbeat on the ultrasound. There was hope! Or so I thought. "My precious angels. Went for my last ultrasound today and they confirmed the passing of my monkeys. Mason is on the left and Alex was no longer visible, but the remnants of his sac are on the right. Even though I never got to meet them, they mean just as much to me as my big girl does. #RIPAlex&Mason #mommyofTHREE" This was the caption of my Instagram post featuring the only picture I would ever have of my babies. This was when it became REAL. I spent many nights crying. I held my baby girl tightly, and I promised her I would never let go. I retreated from the world as much as I could. I knew that God did not take the lives of my babies to punish me, but boy did I think it sometimes.

My doctor was able to tell us the babies' genders based on some blood work that was done at my first appointment. Two boys. Two precious baby boys. The night that we got the news they were boys I had the most vivid dream. My family and I, including our daughter and our sweet baby boys, were fishing. We were all so happy, but in a flash, my boys disappeared. I saw a bright light and my dream transitioned into a field full of wildflowers. In the middle of the field were my babies. Running. Laughing. Playing. Things I would never get to see them do. I woke up from the dream with tears flowing. I immediately knew their names: Mason Andrew and Alexander Mekhi.

I had no symptoms or signs of miscarriage but still my babies were gone. I would never have the chance to hold them, to sing to them, to play with them, to be their mommy. I would never get to experience all of their "firsts." They would never get to hunt and fish with their daddy, or go to the racetrack with their grandfather. They would never get to feel the love that Derek, our daughter, and I had for them.

Discussions began to "help my body along" since I had experienced a missed miscarriage (miscarriage in which the baby, placenta, etc. is not passed naturally). At this point, it was becoming too dangerous to carry the twins much longer due to the risk of infection. I was given the options of either a D&C (Dilation and Curettage), a surgical procedure during which they would essentially dilate my cervix and clean out my uterus in a similar manner to cleaning out the inside of a pumpkin, or to take a pill that would basically put me in labor and I could "deliver" at home. We chose the D&C for the simple fact that I didn't want to have to deal with birthing my babies while trying to care for Lana. I didn't think I was strong enough. Five weeks after my babies passed, December 2, it was time for my surgery. The day came too soon. I wasn't ready.

Usually, when I share my story and people find out how long I carried my babies after they passed, they are shocked. But I am so thankful for that time we had together. God knew EVERY circumstance surrounding my pregnancy. He knew every terrible detail that we would experience. I did not know how, but I knew that He would carry me through this.

The only thing worse than losing my angels, was dealing with the comments that followed:

"Everything happens for a reason."
"At least you already have one."
"God just thought you needed more time with your daughter."
"Well, at least you can still get pregnant."
"There's always next time."

I know people meant well, but these comments were like a stab in my heart EVERY. SINGLE. TIME. I am typically an optimist, but I was having the HARDEST time seeing the silver lining in this situation. Looking back, there is one comment that was sent to me that I didn't understand at the time, but I do now. I was told that while they understood I was hurting, they also knew that my experience would one day allow me to help other women through THEIR experience. And how right they were!

Once it was confirmed that our babies had passed, I made the decision to continue posting about them on all of my social media platforms. But if I'm being honest, I probably wouldn't have been so public about my miscarriage if it weren't for the fact that we had already announced our pregnancy and I couldn't bear to deal with all the questions that would come when the pregnancy didn't end with a beautiful little baby.

I started to fall into a depression. I had dealt with some depression throughout high school, but nothing quite like this. I was TERRIFIED of reaching out and telling someone what I was thinking or feeling at the time. There were nights that I couldn't sleep at all because my head was filled with so many thoughts of what could have been or what I could have done differently to make the pregnancy viable.

Due to the depression, I convinced myself that my mental health was the reason that God took my babies from me. *He already knew that*

I was crazy, I thought to myself. And I believed those thoughts. I let the enemy in, during my most vulnerable time, and I let his lies take hold of me.

Two weeks after my D&C, I looked at my baby girl and realized that God had blessed me tremendously. For almost two whole months, I was so wrapped up in what we had LOST that I had ignored the biggest blessing in our lives. God spoke to me in that moment, and I knew that I had to get back on track. That process HAD to begin with my spiritual life. I bought a new devotional Bible for moms and dove straight in. So many truths were revealed to me in those first few passages, and a new hunger for the Word was birthed.

The more I immersed myself in my studies, the less and less my depression haunted me. I started going to church again. My first Sunday back, the worship team sang "Blessed be the Name of the Lord." To this day, the hook of that song still sends chills over my entire body. As I sang the words, "He gives and takes away, my heart will choose to say, Lord, Blessed be Your name," it was as if I could feel the Father's arms around me. I was flooded with peace and comfort.

Two months and five days after my D&C I found out that we were expecting our rainbow baby. I was immediately filled with fear for the well-being of this baby. We immediately decided that we were NOT going to announce this pregnancy until we at least heard a heartbeat. I prayed harder than I ever had before. And on March 5, 2015, my prayers were answered. My perfect little bean. Healthy. Growing. Alive.

One of my biggest fears about conceiving and birthing our rainbow baby was that I would forget our twins. I was petrified at the thought of losing a grip on what little bit of them I had to hold onto. The legacy of God's faithfulness, that was presented to me through our loss of them and gain of another baby, will FOREVER stand firm and true in my life. The best part about our new baby was that his due date was October 21, 2015. Exactly one year after his big brothers met Jesus. Born a few weeks early, on September 30, my sweet boy, my rainbow, FINALLY arrived.

My big girl was finally a big sister. And I could finally breathe again.

Meeting with Jesus

Heather Blair

I had two miscarriages in the span of eight months while being overseas. My husband and I were living in Beijing at the time and decided to take the plunge into parenthood. What did we have to lose? Little did I know how challenging this would in fact be for us. It is really difficult to put into words what God has done in our lives and hearts through these experiences, but I will try.

Miscarriage #1: February 2013

We had just arrived back to Beijing after visiting my family in Portland. We had decided to have the baby in China. Below are the words of my journal during this time.

February 19, 2013

"Though you have made me see troubles, many and bitter, you will restore my life again; from the depths of the earth you will again bring me up. You will increase my honor and comfort me once again" (Psalm 71:20-21[16]).

I'm not sure where to start. In December we found out we were pregnant and of course were excited. It was really hard to be in China and imagine having the baby here. We just got back from a wonderful visit to Oregon. During our 2nd OB appointment in Beijing, we found out the baby stopped developing at eleven weeks and one day. The heartbeat was not detected and it looks like our baby has died. Not the news we expected to hear but sadly what I was fearful of. I am just so sad and now of course worried about the procedure and future prospects of having children. God, I am not angry with you. In fact, all I can do is just trust you. I don't understand why, but I do know you have a reason. It sucks having to tell everyone and I can't stop crying. This was a fear of mine all along, funny how it actually transpired. What are you wanting me to know? Sure, many women go through this and bounce back to have children, but something could again go wrong with the next child. And again, another operation. Jesus, please please protect me from another operation. I know emotionally you will carry me through that, but how bad it is for my body. There is always something to fear and I'm really good at it. Lead me directly to where I need to be for proper care, Jesus. I want to be handled well during this operation and still have a chance of having babies in the future. I am really just exhausted from crying and not really sure what else to say. I just know that I need your life, comfort and truth! Speak your truth to me above all the lies, loud enough for me to hear. You are the only thing that is constant.

February 23, 2013

I had the operation on Thursday and it's disheartening that I am empty now where there was once a child that you gave to me. I felt very cared for and understood at the hospital. Afterwards, the doctor said he went ahead and had the tissue analyzed to rule out a few causes of death. I don't know what I want to hear and of course I will worry about that. Now seeing from experience, what good does it do to worry anyway? I will just deal with things as they come. I just ask for your peace and comfort in the waiting time and preparation in case something is in fact a problem for us.

This whole situation is really disheartening but I feel at peace with your choices for this baby. I know heaven rejoices to accept this baby and he/she is much better off with you in your arms than the best day here on earth with us. As much as I loved and will continue to love that baby, it doesn't compare to how much you love this baby, Jesus. As I was walking around yesterday, I had a feeling that you were telling me that we are being protected from something. That could be many many things, but you are protecting us from it. I feel comforted at the thought that you know what you are doing. Of course, I knew that all along, but even more so in the moment of clarity yesterday. Who knows if we can have children in the future or if we will continue to have miscarriages or if we can even conceive. I know that will be a difficult reality to face, but you have been through it all and thankfully, Jesus, you are a God that also understands enduring pain. It's scary to think about it now, but I know you are faithful to meet us, walk alongside us, and carry us along the way. There are so many things to be fearful of and I just ask that you make this verse a reality in our lives: "I sought the Lord, and he answered me and delivered me from all of my fears" (Psalm 34:4[17]).

I have experienced so many emotions since we found out we were pregnant. It was excitement of course but also a bit of shock that we were actually doing this. Then I was saddened by the reality that I never realized when my last day of my normal self was and also by the fact that Nathan and I will never be the same again. I then began getting bursts of anxiety and fear, maybe from the hormones, that the baby would die and I would miscarry. From there, something didn't feel quite right. I was just unhappy about our circumstance. The night before we found out our baby died, Nathan and I had a discussion about this. Was I supposed to feel these emotions? Did those emotions play into what happened? Only God really knows and everything will be clear some day in the future, but I do firmly believe you are protecting us from something that is far out of our control. I just praise you for your care in our lives.

"For I know the plans I have for you declares the Lord, plans for welfare and not for evil, to give you a future and a hope." (Jeremiah 29:11[18])

"The Lord is near to the brokenhearted and saves the crushed in spirit. Many are the afflictions of the righteous, but the Lord delivers him out of them all." (Psalms 34:18-19[19])

In all of this, I praise you for your blessings and what I have: health, a loving husband, loving family and friends, and joy in knowing you are with me.

Miscarriage #2: August 2013

I miscarried again at the end of August. Although we were excited about the pregnancy, something didn't feel quite right. This time around, we told very few people about the pregnancy. I didn't want to make a big deal of things until we knew for sure that the baby was fine. I passed the baby at work and tried to stay strong. Nobody knew.

This miscarriage brought a different set of emotions. For one, it was upsetting that we had to go through this again and now the doubt and fear of ever having a child was becoming more of a reality. However, God was faithful in answering our prayers for if this happened again. This time, there was no surgery.

During the first miscarriage, I struggled more with the heartbreak of losing the baby, whereas I struggled more with frustration and fear of the unknown during the second. It felt like every break I had in the day, I was fighting really hard to hold on to truth and God's promises rather than feeling sorry for myself. Then one night, God gave me the most precious experience. I'm still not sure what to call it, a dream? a vision? a meeting? Either way, when I woke up I turned to Nathan and said, "I met with Jesus last night."

When I was asleep, I saw myself suddenly in the presence of Jesus. It was a blinding light so I couldn't see. I knelt down on the ground and covered my face to cry. I wept for the sadness of the babies lost and because of the fear of not knowing if I would bear my own children. In that moment, I felt a warmth around me that brought peace and a sense of calm. Jesus told me, "It's OK. I know. They are with me. I am with you." It was OK to feel the way that I did but He has it under control. He knows the heartbreak I feel. Our babies are with Him and we will meet one day. Whatever happens to us, we will be fine.

He spoke very simple, kind words but each word had a power to comfort and I understood much more than the words themselves. He had the babies though I couldn't see them. There was no prediction that the future would be without trouble but I knew in that moment that we would be fine and that this presence surpasses all earthly happiness.

What I Want

Tracy Kruse

I wanted the babies. I still want them. I have lost two.

Before I lost two babies, I birthed four beautiful children. They, my husband, and I live in Beijing, China. We are blessed with meaningful work; we have good relationships in and outside of our family. All our needs are abundantly supplied. Our first four came to us quite quickly, with all four born in less than three years: a boy, twin boys, and then a girl. Those early years were intensely demanding and difficult, but also sweet and rewarding.

When we married, we said we wanted four-six children. When the first four came so quickly, we decided four was "enough." Then the youngest turned five, life seemed easier again, and we became close friends with a family who had a new baby much younger than their first three. It was so beautiful to watch their older children love and care for their new little one, and watch our *own* children care for and love *their* little one, that we started talking…and dreaming…and suddenly four didn't feel like enough anymore. We thought we might be a little crazy and knew everyone else would be convinced of it, but we decided to just see what happened!

Other than dealing with intense nausea and vomiting neatly contained in the first trimester, my first pregnancies had been, overall, delightful. Even the discomforts of late pregnancy had been precursors to something so wonderful I couldn't really ever bring myself to mind very much. This time began just the same, with the nausea ramping up like clockwork, just like it always had. Impossible to hide, we told our kids with great joy and anticipation very early on that the reason mommy was so sick was because "little sister" would soon be "big sister".

I hate throwing up. But for each pregnancy, every time I would tell myself, *It's for the baby!* and it helped! This was a price I was completely willing to pay for the joy of the precious little one at the end of the journey. The kids grew up and stepped in to help in ways that were so precious. It was easy and priceless to imagine them helping with a newborn. I just couldn't wait!

Even though I was excited about the end of the journey, my severe sickness definitely took its toll on our family, especially on my sweet husband. He had a full plate already, and was now picking up the slack for me. Laser focus on the end kept us going.

Then life began to get harder. Josh had blatant bribery demands and personnel trouble at work. My best local friend, the first I had engaged with in Chinese instead of English, informed me that many of my attempts at loving her well had in fact been hurtful, and she could no longer be my friend. Our landlord informed us he would be selling our apartment and we would need to move. Josh became completely unable to breathe through his nose. Surgery was scheduled to clear his nasal cavity which was completely filled with polyps. We felt like we were barely keeping afloat in the unexpected flood of difficulties.

The day of the surgery prep arrived. The whole family went to the hospital together so I could also hear any important instructions. Since we were already at the hospital and the pregnancy was almost 11 weeks, we decided to do our first prenatal visit! The kids are with us; they can hear the heartbeat. It will be fun!

There's no heartbeat. It's OK; it's still a little early. We'll do a sonogram. There's no heartbeat. The baby is only the size of eight weeks—three weeks too small. We have to immediately explain to our children that what was supposed to be a special "first meeting" has become a nightmare.

The doctor wants to immediately do a D&C. I can't. I won't. Josh is having surgery this week; it's too much. Maybe they're wrong. "Please, God, let them be wrong!!!!" Days pass before I can believe it. I'm still sick. Still throwing up several times a day, but they say the baby is dead. WHY DO I HAVE TO THROW UP IF I DON'T EVEN GET A BABY????? For several days, I mourned the baby I still carried. I wanted to carry it. I didn't want to let it go. How could I still be throwing up if the baby stopped growing nearly a month ago?

Josh's surgery came. While I was in the hospital room waiting for him to return, I noticed spotting for the first time. His surgery was successful, but his first week of recovery was far more painful and difficult than expected.

I was devastated. Our baby was dead. I wasn't much use, but I took care of him and our children the best that I could. Then almost a week later, the bleeding started to increase. We sat down to supper, and I started to feel crampy. I didn't feel like eating. "Crampy" progressed to waves of intense pain, like labor. There was bleeding, passing blood clots. I was still barely able to be upright. Josh found a plastic shower curtain to put down on the floor. I squatted over a bowl, determined to see the baby. I pleaded with God to allow me to see it. The pain became so intense. I was sobbing because it was the hurt of labor without the reward at the end. I felt I just CAN'T anymore. Then I passed several very large blood clots. I felt unexplainably compelled to see the baby. I dug through the clots, but found nothing. After the clots passed, I started to bleed heavily, bleeding through pads in just 5-10 minutes.

I needed to go the emergency room, so we called a dear friend to take me to the hospital because Josh could barely walk to the bathroom without passing out. While I waited for her to get to our home, I went to say goodnight to the children. I was afraid. The bleeding was so heavy. I could feel my life running out of me. Then our oldest son asked, "Will you die?" This is the hardest question motherhood has ever thrown my way! I didn't know how to answer. How could I teach and love my children in this moment when I am genuinely not sure I will ever have an opportunity to do so again? As I pulled them all close, I gave the only answer I knew, "I do not know if God will write 'orphan' into your story but if He does, He is STILL GOOD." I blessed each of them, prayed with them, and then left.

We arrived at the emergency room, a doctor saw me, evaluated me, and asked me to wait for the on-call OB-GYN. While I waited, I went to the bathroom. While there, I passed two more very large clots into the toilet. I could hardly bear it, but I would NOT miss seeing my child and just flush it down the toilet. So I dug the clots out—and found our baby. I washed it gently and then lay it on a paper towel. About an inch long, half head, half body. Ten perfect teensy toes, ten perfect miniscule fingers. Translucent skin, every tiny vertebra visible. Nose and mouth all there, closed, whole. *Fearfully and wonderfully made.* But still so tiny, I will never know if it was a boy or a girl.

After the baby came, the bleeding slowed down to a sustainable level. The ER doctor said we should wait until morning, and as long as it did not increase again, we could go home then. They sent me to the obstetric wing. Many people (including my sweet friend who was at the hospital with me) were apologetic about sending me there but, somehow, I was glad to go. I HAD just birthed a baby. It seemed like the right place to be. I took our tiny little one with me. Studied it, cried over it. Took pictures. Listened to the cries of other newborns and mourned.

"Blessed are those who mourn, for they shall be comforted"(Matthew 5:4[20]). "Blessed be the God and Father of our Lord Jesus Christ, the Father of mercies and God of all comfort, who comforts us in all our affliction, so that we may be able to comfort those who are in any affliction, with the comfort with which we ourselves are comforted by God" (2 Corinthians 1:3-4[21]). These words are *true*. I had not yet lived their truth, but I would.

I went home. I did return to my first four children. And I had one taken away. The Lord gives, and the Lord takes away. But *in the taking away,* He also gave. He gave gifts that could only come in the loss! These are a few of the many gifts I received:

- The opportunity to tell my children in a true time of crisis that *WHATEVER* God writes into their (or my) story, He is good. To LIVE my faith. To test if I believe it, and for them to see that I do.
- To live out our wedding vows. To walk together through a long season of "worse" and prove to each other that when we said, "for better or worse" we really meant it.
- To sit, with my children around me, and cry. To mourn, question and comfort each other.
- To teach my children how to mourn. To, in their presence, be "better" for a while and then be overcome with grief again. To provide a safe place to feel—whatever we feel! To model words and sentences that allow grief to progress in its own time and way. My four children will grieve again. I was given the chance to walk with them closely in their first real experience of loss. When they are older, I will not be allowed so close.
- To experientially, tangibly *know* the Holy Spirit as Comforter.
- To have walked through the darkest thing I could imagine, the loss of a child, and make it to the other side.
- To learn that it is possible to be simultaneously devastated and grateful. To carry anguish and hope together.
- To learn that I am not special. "Why me?" was answered with "Why not me?" Why should others walk painful journeys and not me?
- To see and taste and touch the abundance of care that we received in the weeks following the loss.

77

- The amazing awareness that I am not alone! DOZENS of women that I love and that love me had also walked this journey, and I had no idea!
- The chance to let go of an inappropriate expectation of my husband "understanding" me. We didn't mourn in the same way—and that hurt! He threw himself into his busy schedule, and I wanted to stop everything! Yet in that difference, we were both mourning and dealing with the loss as best we could, and we *could make it to the other side together.*

Each of these gifts is *precious.* I value them. I would so rather have that precious baby. But I am *truly* grateful for the beautiful, life-altering gifts I have been given.

And then, the second time. Surely, the last time was just that "one in five" fluke. It'll be fine. Everyone thought so. Everyone but me. Somehow, I had a much harder time believing that it was true. I wanted to believe that God would give us this baby, but somehow, I was doubtful in my soul from the beginning—scared I would lose this one, too. When the bleeding started, it was simply confirmation. But this time the "why" was stronger. WHAT did I need to learn this time? It was so hard! Why did we even have to get pregnant at all? WHAT WAS I SUPPOSED TO BE LEARNING???? I don't know. I still don't know.

The second time was physically much different from the first time. The first time, after the baby came, I lost weight, looked better than ever, and felt good physically after about a month or so. The second time, I gained more weight, and began a hormonal health roller coaster ride that I still haven't totally finished. The first time, He allowed me to see many of His gifts right away. The second time, it took longer-term faith—without seeing. And yet, now I know, because I have experienced it: *However He writes my story, He is still good.*

I wanted the babies. I still want them. But I want what He has given me: His choice, His story, *Himself,* even more.

Too Wise to Err, Too Good to Be Unkind

Faith Chang

You are too wise to err, and too good to be unkind.
—*Charles Spurgeon*

God is good

I had never prayed from my gut before my second pregnancy. "God, I'll do anything," I pleaded, not hoping to bargain as much as desperately grasping the air for words. "Please, spare our baby." It was early in my first trimester and I was spotting and cramping.

The next day, I lay in my OB-GYN's examining room for an ultrasound. The doctor, studying the screen, said, "I don't like how it looks; this looks like a miscarriage…" Then, mercifully, "Wait, I think I see a heartbeat." And in the brief pause between the news of miscarriage and of life, God gave me a foretaste of the otherworldly peace he gives to his children, even as our greatest fears seem to materialize.

The months to follow were fraught with graphic nightmares of pregnancy loss and sleep-robbing anxiety, but slowly and surely, wonderfully and fearfully, our second child was fashioned within me.

"We learned that smaller animals or people have faster heartbeats than bigger animals or people," she recounted to me recently, detailing her trip to the science museum. And I wonder at how our articulate, expressive four-year-old is the one whose fluttering heart was barely detected at five weeks in-utero. God has been good to me.

God is kind

God is kind. I believed it, even as I mourned, even as I wept for our newest little one, my third baby, who we'd only seen on a tiny black-and-white screen, whose presence I'd only known by my all-day "morning" sickness.

Once again there had been cramping and spotting, but the first ultrasound was different this time. I again pleaded we'd see the sweet flickering of a heartbeat, but there was none. I scheduled another appointment and was sent home to wait.

At home, I prayed with my husband for the privilege of meeting and raising our yet unborn child. Our parents prayed for their unborn grandchild and our siblings for their niece or nephew. We hoped and we waited.

But the next two ultrasounds showed no signs of fetal growth. In the same room that I first tasted God's perfect peace in a doctor's brief pause, God was with me as I talked through medical decisions regarding the miscarriage.

In the weeks to follow, the truth of God's kindness carried a force within my heart I had never known before. Even in weeping for our unborn child—not merely over a lost hope or imagined future, but the death of our precious one—as I cried out, "My baby, my baby," with grief that surprised and rocked me, God was never unkind. He was gentle, lavish with love through His people, and clear in comfort from His word. I felt His nearness and found solace in the description of our Savior as a man familiar with sorrows. I rested in knowing my little one was in the presence of God, who enabled me to worship in my pain.

I found that even in grief, my faith was upheld by the One who is faithful and true. So I journaled, not wanting to forget his loving kindness and comfort in our loss:

December 3, 2015

> *As I write, my body for the last two days has been responding to what it knows via hormone levels and other channels mysterious to me—that our third child is no longer here and will not need the home he or she had been struggling to live in for the past six weeks…God has been kind as the cramping as of now is not too bad and the bleeding moderate, but He has been kind in many other ways. More than that, He has been speaking many truths to our hearts:*

> **The comfort of His loving kindness.** *That He wills for us to know Him as kind, gentle, and good takes away the image of Him as "loving" in a bring-the-best-result, but in a cold or calculating way. Psalm 103 and the meditations I've had on it all of last week have been my reference point.*

> **The image of His strong hands.** *Nothing and no one can pry our baby out of His loving, strong hands. Not us. Not death or the powers of hell. Death did not steal him or her away. God held and brought our precious one through the door of death into life.*

> **We will meet soon.** *This is the first time the fleeting nature of our lives (Psalm 103) has been a comfort to me. Life here is short, but his love is from everlasting to everlasting for us and for our children's children. On the other side, when we meet, we will together glorify God,*

whose wisdom and paths are unsearchable and beyond full comprehension. Then this separation will feel light and momentary as it truly is.

This is not a tragedy. *To be delivered straight into glory. To not have to wrestle with indwelling sin or grieve the effects of the fall. To not have to see but through a mirror dimly lit—but to behold the glory of God, to be captured by His beauty without wrestling with doubt and self-love, to be with Christ—that is far, far better. There is no comparison. Baby Chang is drinking deeply of eternal, all-satisfying joy beyond comprehension. He or she is privileged to behold things mom and dad now only know by faith.*

How that veil between here and there seems so much thinner. Heaven so much closer and nearer. Not that we long for our baby more than our truest treasure—but knowing what we long for is being beheld already by one of our own. Perhaps we will be learning much from this little one when we meet again.

This suffering has been entrusted to us and our faith is revealed. *I don't know how else to express it, except in the midst of all this it feels in some ways as if a privilege has been given to us. This is not a club I would have asked to join or a trial I would have chosen. However, our faith is coming forth, shown to be strong because of him. Shown to be precious and true, relevant and reliable. This is because our God is all that (precious, true, relevant, reliable) to the uttermost.*

Shall we take the good from God and not the evil? (Job 2:10) I felt this question on Tuesday night, in the midst of feeling cramping, sitting in the bathroom as my sweet girl sat in the tub and sang "Bless the Lord." How could I receive my daughters as good from God's hand but refuse to receive trials too? Both come from his fatherly hand in all wisdom and deep compassion and kindness.

Our hope is sure and steadfast. Not sentimentalism. Not wishful thinking. But anchored in Christ—His Person and Word. And that has been everything to us.

Our sweet baby, in his or her short life, taught us so much of God. With one girl name and one boy name picked out, we don't know yet which name to go by. So we refer to this little one by the middle name we've chosen—Pax, meaning "peace." Deep sadness and profound peace are often woven mysteriously together in the believer's darkest nights, and we experienced both with Pax.

God is wise

"I think I'm depressed," I texted a friend. It was not yet four months since the miscarriage. There were two new toddlers in our home and another round of morning sickness. This time though, I didn't feel the sweet assurance of God's kindness toward me, even with the gift of new life now burgeoning in my womb. There was the stress of foster care and special needs, nausea and fatigue, and a persistent, pervasive aching in my heart.

It can be a bit difficult to explain how you can miss someone you've never met face to face. But carrying a child in your womb is profoundly intimate and you do not need to have first held a child in your arms to have loved deeply and fiercely. We loved each of our babies from the moment we learned of their presence. I missed Pax.

A stomach bug passing through the whole family and a toddler screaming out in the middle of the night pushed me over the edge. *God, don't You know that I can't handle this?* I prayed as I lay in bed exhausted and anxious. And then, for the first time, *God, are you really being good to me?*

In the months that followed, the truths I knew of God set boundaries for my thoughts and heart. His word kept me from wandering too far into dangerous places. However, none of Scripture's promises about his purposes in suffering resounded to bring comfort. It was hard, it didn't feel worth it, and the worst thing was that God didn't seem near.

Our God in his kindness stoops down to deal gently with his struggling and angry children. And in the midst of another difficult night, He brought to mind Job. Job, who in all his terrible loss, and even after speaking to God face-to-face, never saw the full purposes of his suffering in his lifetime. He never knew his story was unfolding in front of an audience in the spiritual realms. He couldn't have fathomed the believers in millennia to come who would behold God in their own trials through the most painful moments of his life. He was simply and powerfully asked, by God himself, if he would surrender to his wisdom and ways.

I was being asked the same. If I were to see things as God does, if I could trace even a thread of his purposes in our story down into eternity, I would fall to my knees in awe and joyful worship. Would I take hold of this by faith? By God's grace I wanted to. With His help I would choose to trust. With trust came increasing measures of rest for my soul.

God, the wise and kind Giver

The year after the miscarriage, I was again asked to surrender my need to understand; to trust God's kindness and wisdom not in trial, but in blessing. Our son's name means *"God heals,"* and his presence has been God's gracious balm to my heart. Born one year after Pax, his presence does not negate the sadness of our loss. But my capacity for joy, it seems, has been made greater through sorrow. More than ever before, my smiles are accompanied with grateful tears.

As I cradled my son in the hours after his birth, I found myself wondering at it all. *Why such blessing, God?* I would pull him close, kiss the top of his little head, breathe in his sweet baby smell and I couldn't understand. *Why this great kindness to us? Why such a good gift in the midst of such suffering around me and in the world?* Simply because He is a good God and He gives good gifts, His word tells me (James 1:17). Our son is one of His good gifts and our Good Giver's ways are beyond me. So again, I am being asked to trust His wisdom.

I will never fully comprehend the ebb and flow of God's giving and taking away, of good gifts and needful trials. And because I don't understand, I am tempted to question. I am apt to offer fumbling human explanations for why He does what He does or to become anxious about what trials lie ahead. But God…He is too wise to err. He is too good to be unkind.

In our bedroom, next to our bed sits the crib of our youngest son. On our dresser top is a framed ultrasound of his older sibling whom we have yet to meet. Our Father is infinitely wise, rich in steadfast love, and perfect in all His ways. In trial and in blessing, God has been wise and He has been kind. Therefore, in surrender and thanks, not understanding it all, I praise. With a baby boy snuggled in my arms and another precious one in the presence of God, I praise:

Oh, the depth of the riches and wisdom and knowledge of God! How unsearchable are His judgments and how inscrutable His ways!

"For who has known the mind of the Lord,
or who has been His counselor?"
"Or who has given a gift to Him that He might be repaid?"
For from Him and through Him and to Him are all things.
To Him be glory forever.
Amen.
(Rom 11:33-36[22])

The Letter

Temi

My dear child,

I love you more than you know. I hope you are deeply buried in His bosom. I imagine you smiling and laughing completely oblivious to your near arrival into my life. I know you are loved by Him but it is important to me that you know you are loved by me always. It would be untrue to say that I talk about you often or at all but when I see a newborn baby every now and then I do think about you. For a few moments, I imagine what it would be like to hold you close. I wonder if you'd be just like your big sister, playful and energetic!

Sometimes in those moments, I am disappointed that I couldn't muster the faith to fight for you like I did for your sister; if I did, you'd be three today. There was a time I had no desire for children. Broodiness did not come naturally and then one day like snow in March you showed up on a pee stick...Just like that! I was frightened and excited all at the same time.

Against all logic and good advice I told everyone who cared to listen under the guise of small talk you'd be joining us soon. By week three, I was walking around the house pushing my tummy out and practicing being uncomfortable and difficult. I strapped my baby on board badge to my chest like a medal of honor and complained shamelessly about how tired I was even when I wasn't. Really, I just loved carrying you inside me. I couldn't wait to see the best thing Isaac and Temi would ever produce. It was all planned. I could already see you running around the house, backchatting and correcting my grammar. My mini-me.

I knew you would be amazing and couldn't wait to meet you. The day before our first scan was very normal. I returned from work in London. Your dad as always made dinner. We made love, fell asleep and an hour later I could feel you leaving me. Your daddy cleaned up all the blood, bathed me and put me to sleep.

I did not pray. I could not pray. I also did not grieve. Grief is a response to a sense of loss. I own nothing so I can lose nothing. Yes, you are not with me now but I am convinced we will meet again.

"For I am convinced that neither death nor life, neither angels
nor demons neither the present, nor the future, nor any powers
neither height nor death nor anything else in creation, will be
able to separate us from the love of God that is in Jesus Christ."
(Romans 8:38-39[23])

Fearfully and Wonderfully Made

Gloria Crawford

For as long as I can remember, I hoped to be a mom. I imagined myself being a mom of four, two boys and two girls—even numbers so that there's always someone to ride with when you're at Disneyland.

Terry and I met in Beijing, three weeks before he moved to Hong Kong to start his first law job. We got married a year and a half later, and in less than three months, we found ourselves pregnant with our firstborn son! While earlier than we had planned, we were excited to start our family and incorporated parenthood into our honeymoon phase. Our philosophy was, now that we've started, let's pop them out and get things going! We knew that living abroad was something we wanted to do, and with the potential of moving around, we wanted our kids to have built-in friends wherever we ended up.

When Trey was three months old, our little family moved to New York City. About a year later, Sean joined the bunch, and the four of us enjoyed the adventures of urban family living on the Upper West Side. When the whole extended family visited us for Christmas nine months later, we surprised everyone with the news that the Crawford family was growing yet again.

A few weeks later, Terry got a call from a headhunter about an opportunity in Beijing too good to pass up. We had done the transpacific move before, and while we were sad to say goodbye to the life we had built in New York, we looked forward with anticipation to returning to the city where we first met. By this time, pregnancy was old hat. I hadn't worn normal clothes in two years and operating on odd eating and sleeping schedules was the norm. When the time came for my twelve-week prenatal appointment, I told Terry, "You don't need to come. It's just routine and I'll bring the ultrasound picture home for you."

After a few minutes in the ultrasound room, the technician told me that she would be right back. She had already shown me the heartbeat and printed out a profile picture that I could take home. I remember thinking, *Could we please speed this along? I've got two little boys waiting for me at home!* It didn't cross my mind that anything could be wrong until a new doctor came in and asked if my husband was here. The next few minutes were a blur. "…Neural tube defect…acrania…skull did not develop…brain tissue is being exposed to amniotic fluid…do you want to call your husband?" All I could do was nod. It was as if my body and brain were on autopilot. I called Terry and said, "Um, something is wrong with the baby. Can you come?" I then proceeded to follow a nurse while she told me about coming back the next day for a D&C procedure.

Terry arrived as I sat down in my OB-GYN doctor's office. He started asking questions, "What happens if we decide to carry to term?" My doctor had never been asked this question before. "Well, even if the baby survived, it wouldn't be a 'good' baby." At that point, I was broken out of my shocked state. How could anyone dictate whether or not my baby was a 'good' baby? We graciously told the doctor that we couldn't make any decisions today and would go home to think about things.

As soon as I got home, I scoured the internet for any information I could find about acrania and anencephaly. Deep down, I hoped and hoped for some information that would make me feel better about termination. Instead, I came across several heartbreaking yet inspirational stories of other families carrying their precious ones to term. Terry and I had both dealt with the loss of a family member before, but this was different. I wrestled with God, "I'd almost rather just say goodbye now. How am I going to deal with six more months of questions and grieving before I've actually experienced loss?"

We called my sister and a best friend. They both came over right away. We cried together. We prayed together. Terry and I came away knowing that this wasn't our call to make.

All of this happened the day before Terry's last day at his firm. Our move to Beijing was already set into motion. After getting a second opinion from another OB-GYN (where we found out we were carrying a baby girl) and an appointment with a pediatric neurosurgeon, we confirmed that there would be no additional risk to my health, nor would the baby suffer in the womb as the pregnancy continued. As a result, we felt like the most life-affirming choice for us would be to move forward with our move and trust God with the ultimate result.

We wrote to our friends around the world: "We obviously have a tremendous number of things to request prayer about: six months ahead of us during which Gloria's pregnancy will likely continue, an imminent move and period of adjustment to China, a new and challenging job, and most daunting, a very emotionally difficult birth. We of course believe that God can provide a miracle should He desire, and as a result we are trying to strike the balance between praying boldly and preparing for what is most likely…We are most thankful for how we are learning to trust more and more in the God who also knew in advance that He was going to lose a child."

For the next few weeks, I was almost afraid to get attached. Part of me was just going through the motions of doing what I felt was obedient. I prayed for a miracle, knowing that we serve a God who is powerful enough to perform one, but also having reserved and realistic expectations. Then God introduced us to a radiologist who said to me, "This is the one chance you get to spoil your child without any negative ramifications." He proceeded to tell us how beautiful our baby girl was and how all she would ever know was unconditional love—our love as her parents and then straight to her heavenly Father's love. At that moment, I realized that my current job and calling was to love my baby. So we named her Kaly (a derivation of Kalila, which means "precious loved one").

God went before us. We couldn't have planned our arrival to Beijing any better. My roommate from Beijing back when I met Terry for the first time had just moved back to Beijing with her husband six months before us. They paved the way for us. We ended up moving into their same apartment complex and fell into a community of support.

One of the things I was most anxious about before the move was having to explain my situation over and over to people who wouldn't understand. I knew it would be such a cultural paradigm shift, even for those who knew God. My very first OB-GYN appointment in Beijing was with a Chinese doctor. We were still in the midst of deciding where we would be delivering, and since I had already gone through two pregnancies, I really just wanted to do a quick checkup to make sure my blood pressure and blood sugar levels were normal. The doctor looked at me sternly and said, "You know there's a problem, right?" I tried not to break into tears and explained that I knew and still wanted to carry to term. "Why would you put your body through that trauma if you know it's not going to turn out well?" I half-heartedly tried to explain that I loved her just the same as my other children, but mostly bit my tongue while I drank that awful sugary drink for my blood glucose test.

A couple of days later, I received a call. "Hello, my name is Beverly and I'm calling from BJU." I immediately responded with a cheerful, "Are you calling to tell me I have gestational diabetes?" (I was expecting this, as I had had gestational diabetes with Sean). I heard a sigh of relief on the other end of the line. "Are you able to handle that additional piece of news?" She sweetly introduced herself as the quality assurance supervisor for the OB-GYN department of the hospital and asked if there was anything she could do to assist us. "Also, I noticed that you marked 'Christian' on your patient intake form. Are you plugged into a small group? I go to the international church here and would be happy to introduce you to some people to support you during this time."

Once again, God provided just what I needed right at the exact time I needed it. Beverly became an advocate for me and introduced me to Dr. Brooks, the head of the OB-GYN department with thirty-five years of experience. He respected our decision to carry to term, reassured us that we could deliver naturally, and was sympathetic to our case. He reminded us that we were in China, so he couldn't guarantee that we wouldn't get an awkward question or comment through the process, but he and Beverly worked together to train the staff to be more sensitive. "It will be good for them to see this, since they rarely see or even hear about such cases." A couple of months before Kaly arrived, our case was selected for a perinatal conference where obstetricians, pediatricians, and outpatient and inpatient nurses met together to better understand how to support our family and others going through similar cases in the future. We were told afterwards that there was good discussion regarding value and respect of others' views even when they are different from those they hold. *I have a strong sense that as you labor and deliver that your room will be a "holy ground" with a palpable sense of the Father's presence.* I continue to praise God for his provision of these encouraging words from Beverly while we waited in anticipation.

The boys were young. Trey was two and a half, and Sean was just a little over one when I started showing. For a while, it seemed like Sean thought Kaly was my belly button. Whenever we would say, "Where's Kaly?" Sean would lift my shirt and touch my belly button. We told the boys that a baby was coming, and that we needed to pray for her because "her head was broken." We told them that God was big enough to heal her, but that if He didn't, it wasn't because He loved us any less, and that He wanted her to be in heaven with Him…and that she would be so happy there. To this day, I often think about how our boys' eternal perspective began to take shape then.

As Kaly grew and I grew larger, others excitedly shared in our anticipation. "When are you due?" "It is a boy or a girl?" How much I divulged depended upon where I thought our relationship might go. Some days, I was more emotional than others, but amazingly, I found myself able to celebrate Kaly's life in the small ways. Often there were no words that could be said. However, sometimes God would bring something unexpected and wonderful in the form of words and revelations from others. One afternoon, some dear Chinese friends of mine told me, "Your family is deeply blessed. Blessed to be a part of a legacy of believers. Blessed to have seen God's faithfulness in trials past. Blessed to be able to carry Kaly to term. Blessed to love and be loved. Kaly has already experienced more love from her parents, siblings, aunties, and uncles than many others do in a lifetime."

Many unknowns continued to swirl in our thoughts and hearts. We had no idea if Kaly would be born alive, and it was difficult to imagine what the time would be like if we had any with her outside the womb. I was faced with the conflicting emotions of wanting the pregnancy to be over, yet never wanting it to end. Kaly moved so much more than the boys, which may have been a special blessing for us in learning how to enjoy the here and now, and we did our best to enjoy her as much as possible in the womb. Kaly got to visit the Great Wall, and even attended a men's volleyball match at the Olympics.

On August 15, 2008, Kaly Grace Crawford arrived at 5:30 PM weighing 2.995 kg and measuring 48 cm long. She came out sputtering and gave a little cry as the doctor handed her over to me. She had lots of black hair, and when she opened one eye, we saw that it was blue. The pediatrician on call came in to do a quick check, and as he left the room, he gave us a big smile and said, "You guys are great!"

When Dr. Brooks handed Kaly to me, I was so happy to hold her, and at the same time felt it so surprisingly easy to let her go. Seeing her obvious condition made me want to let her go home to Jesus and get her new body. I said to her, "Kaly girl, thank you so much for staying alive and saying hi to us. You can go home to Jesus now because you need to go get whole. This is not the way it's supposed to be."

Kaly was with us for eight hours. The timing of her arrival was perfect for the boys to come and meet her. Neither of the boys noticed Kaly's appearance. They both said, "Baby!" and tried to touch her face. The staff at the hospital were wonderful. They put us away from the maternity ward so that we could have more privacy and left us alone so that I didn't have anyone rushing me to say goodbye. That night, Kaly went home to be with Jesus while I held her in my arms.

There were special blessings the next day. When the family came to the hospital, Trey looked around, and then came over to give me some extra snuggles. It was as if he remembered what I had said to him, that Kaly would hopefully come and say hello to the family, and then go to heaven to see Jesus. He didn't ask where she was, and he just leaned his head on my chest, as if to comfort me. That evening, we had a simple memorial service and were blessed to have our friends celebrate Kaly's short but very impactful life with us.

The tears continued to come and go, particularly with the aches and pains of the physical recovery without a baby to hold. But overall, God had brought such peace and hope to our family, a steady comfort that did not waver.

We can cry with hope
We can say goodbye with hope
'Cause we know our goodbye is not the end
And we can grieve with hope
'Cause we believe with hope
There's a place where we'll see your face again
We'll see your face again
—Steven Curtis Chapman ("With Hope")

About seven months later, Terry and I found ourselves back at Beijing United Family Hospital. The ultrasound technician turned to us and said, "Everything looks great." We said, "Are you sure?" She looked at us quizzically, then looked back at my medical records. "Oh! Yes, definitely everything is OK—here's her head." As soon as I realized it was another girl, a wave of emotion came over me. God had gifted me with what I had always hoped for—two boys, and two girls.

Terry and I have always prayed that God would use each of our family members to impact our small sphere of influence. He certainly did that through Kaly in a powerful way. Her story continues to encourage so many from different cultures, different languages, different walks. I pray that you too are encouraged by her story.

Beyond the "M" Word

Pamela Djima

When I was pregnant with my first child, I spent the first trimester working a full-time job and two part-time jobs. This meant that I was working well over forty hours a week. Right before I left my main job, my husband and I flew to the US and took a road trip from Seattle to Montana in order to attend the wedding of our friends. After the wedding, we jetted back to China, I completed my employment contract and then we flew home to England for my brother in law's wedding. I came back to Beijing, taught at a summer camp and then went backpacking around Thailand and Laos with my husband. During this trip, I rode an elephant, travelled across the country on an overnight train and endured a two-day boat journey that often felt like it would never end. We topped all this off with a long-distance bus journey that spiralled into a seventeen-hour ordeal after the air conditioning went kaput and the bus was stuck behind another vehicle that had broken down.

I rode a bicycle throughout the entire pregnancy, I ate raw salmon (before I knew that pregnant people aren't supposed to do that) and I didn't start taking prenatal vitamins until after the third trimester. Despite all of this, our first child, a beautiful baby girl, was born in February 2015—healthy and whole with nothing broken and nothing missing. Our daughter was conceived approximately one month after we decided to start "trying for a baby."

I think the smoothness and relative ease of this conception and pregnancy led me to take reproduction for granted. I knew what a miscarriage was and I knew it happened to some but I never envisioned that it would ever be a part of my story.

For as long as I can remember, I have wanted four children as close in age as possible (but not quadruplets). I have an older sister who is just one year, two weeks, and one day older than I am. She is a dear friend who has helped to shape me into the person I am today. This relationship is one of the things that led me to conclude that the closer my children are in age the greater the chance that they will be great friends.

I discovered I was pregnant for the second time when my daughter was seven months old. My husband and I were elated. All this changed approximately two months later. I had been feeling fine, and to my knowledge, the pregnancy was progressing without a hitch. One evening I went to the toilet, wiped and there was blood. Due to the uneventful nature of my first pregnancy, I wasn't particularly alarmed. Then there was more blood and then more. My husband decided that it was time to see a doctor.

So, off we went to the hospital—my husband, our nine-month-old daughter, and myself. As they prepared me for the ultrasound, I tried hard to believe that everything would be well. It was a Chinese hospital and the ultrasound team was not in any way competent in English. Shortly after the technician began moving the transducer across my stomach, I could tell that something was wrong. There were two members of staff in the room with us and both of them started making confused sounds as the device was frantically moved around my stomach. Eventually, one of the ladies uttered four words. They were spoken in imperfect English but their meaning was crystal clear—"Your baby no grow."

As I reflected on the news we had just received and played out the implications, I thought back to my first pregnancy. I think the intrepid nature of that pregnancy helped me not to blame myself for the way this pregnancy had developed. When I made comparisons, I was a lot more adventurous when I was carrying my first child and yet the result of that pregnancy was very different from this one.

I remember just wanting to know why. I asked the doctors. I asked the nurses. I asked the ultrasound team. They threw out various postulations. I was informed that it could be because I was breastfeeding. I was also told that it could be because of the bad air in Beijing. None of these "answers" satisfied my soul. I actually still do not know what caused the loss but about a year and a half later, I was reassured by a kind doctor who repeatedly declared that it was not my fault. "We're not God," she gently told me, "We don't have all the answers." I don't know if that doctor was a Christian but I did find peace in her words.

I don't pretend to have all the answers, but there are some things that I am sure of. I know that God is a good God and the giver of life. I also know that it is His delight to give good gifts to his children. I understand that the devil comes to kill, steal and destroy and I'm convinced that Jesus came to give abundant life. I do not believe that a loving God would give me a good gift and then end the life of the baby while he or she was still in my womb.

As we sat in the back of a taxi on our way home from the hospital, we were driven down a road that I must have walked down a hundred times before. We passed an abandoned shop that had the metal shutters pulled down. I noticed that somebody had spray-painted the words HOPE in big, colorful graffiti. I had never noticed that before. When we got home, I laid down for a nap beside my daughter; I always found that comforting. I slept deeply. When we woke up, my daughter came and stood beside me as I sat on the bed. She put her hand on my shoulder; it was a tender touch. Once again, I was being comforted by Hope.

That day was a Wednesday, the day we held our weekly small group gathering. I did not want to host that evening but somehow we found the strength to honor our commitment. During the prayer request part of the meeting, we shared the doctor's report with those that were present. Our small group consisted of a group of university students, none of whom were married or had children. Many of them were teenagers and the rest were in their early twenties. It seemed as if their world was so far removed from ours. We laid bare our hearts and asked for prayer. We had decided to believe for a miracle. Many of the students volunteered to pray for us. I will never forget the sweet young lady who eventually did. She began by saying something along the lines of, "One of the reasons we praise and worship you is because you conquered death and rose from the grave!" This wasn't a safe "Lord, if it is your will" type of prayer. Her words were full of boldness and authority. That evening, we felt that we were among brothers and sisters who were standing in faith beside us. I saw God in that.

The doctor told us to wait between one and three months to begin trying for another baby. By the end of the next month, I was pregnant. The "kids" in our small group were some of the first people that we shared our news with. When we told them, the group erupted in jubilation. Our second daughter was born in September 2016—healthy and whole with nothing broken and nothing missing. Things were looking good. Being a mother of two was challenging but so rewarding.

When my second daughter was seven months old, we found out that I was pregnant again. We were delighted. This was what we wanted. The baby was due before our oldest daughter would be three. So we would have had a 0-year-old, a 1-year-old, and a 2-year-old. It might seem trivial to some but I always thought that would be pretty cool. I have had to let that dream go.

I started bleeding around the beginning of June. I went to the toilet one morning, wiped and saw blood. My heart sank. I purposed to walk in faith. However, as the days progressed the bleeding continued. We eventually decided to go to the hospital. I remember the date because it was the day that my youngest daughter was exactly ten months old. I left my two daughters at home with my husband and headed to the hospital.

This time the ultrasound was different. I could see the fetal sack but I could also see what looked like a black blob inside of it. "What's that?" I asked in Chinese. "Your baby," the nurse responded in English. The baby was perfectly still; there was no movement whatsoever. "What's wrong?" I asked. "Your baby is dead," came the response.

Just as I had done with the first loss, I marched off to an international hospital for a second opinion. This was the hospital that our first daughter was born in. Maybe subconsciously, I regard that infirmary as a place of hope because every time I've sought positivity in the midst of such terrible news I've found myself there.

At the international hospital, I accosted the foreign doctor in the hallway. I told her that I really needed to speak with her about a matter of great urgency. She looked confused but nevertheless she ushered me into her office. We both sat while I explained the situation to her. As I articulated myself in my native tongue, I experienced the liberation that comes from fully understanding and being fully understood. Part way through my explanation I became overwhelmed with sorrow and broke down in tears. It was as if the realization of what was happening hit me at that very moment. The doctor handed me tissues and offered me kind comfort. This was the same doctor who told me that because we are not God we do not have all the answers.

I explained that at the other hospital the doctors were adamant that I needed to have an operation to remove the baby from my womb as soon as possible. I did not know then and I still do not really know now all that such an operation entails but I knew for certain that I wanted no part of it. The doctors at the Chinese hospital had told me that the baby was too big to pass through my body without assistance. The physician that now sat before me scanned the ultrasound documentation that I had handed her and promptly announced that what I had been told was untrue. "Don't rush into anything," she advised, "Wait one week and then repeat the scan." As I prepared to leave I paused to enquire about payment for the consultation. "So, I pay at the front desk, right?" The kind doctor asked if I had signed in. I told her that I had not. She said, "You're supposed to sign in when you arrive." Then she smiled and said, "It's OK. Just go." That evening the baby left my womb "naturally." I experienced strong contractions before the dead life slipped out of my body.

One of the worst things about having a miscarriage is having to go back to people and tell them that actually the situation has changed. I often struggled with how to phrase this news. I don't like the word "miscarriage." I think it's because it's such a loaded word, full of such pain and disappointment. I often searched for a more poetic way to communicate, a way that involved using less direct words. I would say something like, "The baby is no more" or "there was no heartbeat" or in response to a direct question about the pregnancy, "Oh yeah, that didn't end well."

One of my biggest concerns was regarding all of the people that we had already told about the pregnancy. In particular, I wondered what I would say to my non-Christian clients. I was concerned that it was going to look as if God was not faithful and had failed to come through for us. What words would I use to articulate what had happened? After spending some time agonizing over this, I received a remarkable revelation—I am not God's public relations officer. God needs no defense or no defender. He is God all by Himself. As a witness, I am called only to tell of what I know. All I could do was communicate what happened. I could try my best to cast the events in the light of Christ but ultimately I had very little control over the deductions that were drawn. I could not connect the dots in people's hearts or lead them to the desired inference. I had to trust that God can and does speak to people and that He is able to lead them to the right conclusions about Himself.

I witnessed this firsthand particular client. A while after I shared my experience with her, she confided in me that she had recently discovered that she was pregnant. The pregnancy was completely unexpected. Not long after learning that she was pregnant, she lost the baby. This was fresh news and the emotions were still raw. She was still recovering from the operation that she had had in relation to this. This isn't information that people usually share with their child's tutor.

I saw God in the fact that she was willing to open up to me and show such vulnerability. I know God did not cause either of us to lose our babies but I do wonder if she would have ever felt comfortable enough to be so open if I hadn't shared with her about my own pregnancy and subsequent loss.

A single lady who desperately wanted to be married once told me that she found it very difficult to attend weddings. I listened politely but I couldn't actually relate to what she was saying. Now I can. Not long after my last loss, I spotted a pregnant woman outside my apartment complex. Now, it wasn't that I wanted her to not be pregnant; it was just that the sight of her reminded me of what I wanted and did not have.

Later on, I confessed to a friend that I was jealous of pregnant women. She told me many things but one of the things I clearly remember her saying was that she had felt the same way when she and her husband were struggling to conceive. I felt that someone else could empathize with how I was feeling. I also found that once I had vocalized my negative feelings they were no longer as strong. I regard this as an example of the sense of solidarity and internal healing that are sparked by honest sharing.

After both losses, I was conscious of a great sense of shame. I felt as if I had failed at some very important task. My feeling was compounded by the fact that my failure was not secret. *How can I walk with my head held high after this?* I thought. I was reminded of how I felt after failing my driving test (I actually failed the test six times). Informing people of the loss was reminiscent of sharing the news that I had failed my driving test. Only this was so much more significant. I could not simply practice more and make another booking at my convenience. I had a lot less control over this situation and what was at stake was of far greater value than a UK driving license.

I did not blame God for either of the losses and I never felt anger towards Him. I always knew that God was for me and not against me. I did feel anger but this anger was directed at the devil. I had such a tangible sense of having had something precious stolen from me. I didn't want to adopt the posture of a passive victim. I wanted to somehow fight back. I felt compelled to do a study on what exactly it was that Jesus' death on the cross made available for us. I reflected on the believer's authority and what exactly it means to "speak to the mountain." I was encouraged by what I learned and began to put these truths into practice.

In the aftermath, I was very aware of just how unfair the whole situation was. I remember lamenting to my husband, "Hordes of women get pregnant (and stay pregnant) who don't even want to be pregnant and some of them even kill their babies as they are growing inside them! But I actually wanted to be pregnant and have this baby, how comes I don't get to carry this baby to full term?" The conclusion that I came to is this: Yes, life really is unfair. We live in a fallen and imperfect world and unjust things happen on a regular basis. What a dismal realization that would be if that was the end of the story. But that is not the end of the story. The truth is there is a God and if we entrust our lives to Him, He really will do right by us. This does not mean that I will get everything I want, when I want it and how I want it. What it means is that even though I walk through the valley of the shadow of death, I can trust that I am not alone. God has my life in His hands and His plans for me are for good and not evil.

As I write this piece, I am pregnant with my third child. Or I could say I am pregnant with my fifth child since the two babies that were lost were also my children. In any case, my two daughters will soon have a new sibling to love and cherish. The due date of my last loss has not yet passed and so I do still think about what could have been and what it would have been like to birth a baby at that time. We have booked a holiday for around that period. An exotic vacation does not in any way compare with bringing a human life into the world, but I think this is a small way for me to turn something negative into a positive. I know with my first loss I wanted to do something significant the month that that baby would have been born. I think it is a way to ensure that the losses do not feel like such a waste.

With the baby that I am now carrying, we decided to do things a bit differently. We told our loved ones earlier than usual that I was pregnant. For me this was a real act of faith. After two losses, it would have been easy to have feared the worst. However, I decided to reject fear and trust God. And so here I am, waiting with great anticipation to welcome another child into our family. I am very conscious that the baby that is growing inside of me is a good gift from God and I am so very grateful. I am choosing to trust that this pregnancy will go well and that next year we will meet our new child—healthy and whole with nothing broken and nothing missing.

Endnotes

[1]   AMP
[2]   NKJV
[3]   AMP
[4]   NASB
[5]   NASB
[6]   NIV
[7]   NIV
[8]   NKJV
[9]   NIV
[10] AKJV
[11] NIV
[12] NIV
[13] NIV
[14] NIV
[15] ESV
[16] NIV
[17] ESV
[18] ESV
[19] ESV
[20] NKJV
[21] ESV
[22] ESV
[23] NIV